the story of British english

J. N. HOOK

Professor of English, Emeritus
University of Illinois at Urbana

Scott, Foresman and Company • Glenview, Illinois

Dallas, Tex. • Oakland, N.J.

Palo Alto, Cal. • Tucker, Ga. • Brighton, England

CONTENTS

siblings cousins and ancestors

1. Brothers and Sisters of
the English Language

Most languages, like the people who use them, exist in families. English is one member of the world's largest family of languages, called the Indo-European family.

A member of a family may have siblings (brothers and sisters), cousins, and older relatives such as parents (and their siblings), grandparents, great-grandparents, and so on, back as far as the family tree can be traced. A member of a language family may have similar groups of relatives. In this section we'll look at some of the languages that may be considered the brothers and sisters of English.

Let's begin by counting to ten in English and Dutch. Then we'll add German and Danish.

English	Dutch	German	Danish
one	een		
two	twee		
three	drie		
four	vier		
five	vijf (sounds like "veef")		
six	zes		
seven	zeven		
eight	acht		
nine	negen		
ten	tien		
. . .			
hundred	honderd		

Although none of the numbers are exactly alike, the similarities between the English and Dutch are so great that chance alone could hardly account for them.

► Copy the English and Dutch numbers on a sheet of paper, and then add the corresponding German and Danish numbers by unscrambling these two lists:

German: sieben, hundert, drei, sechs, acht, zehn, eins, vier, neun, fünf, zwei (German z sounds like "ts")

Danish: to, syv, fire (sounds like "fee-ruh"), tre, seks, otte, ni, ti, hundrede, en, fem

Note the similarities in the four lists.

We could add other lists from Swedish, Norwegian, Icelandic, Plattdeutsch (the colloquial Low German of northern Germany), and Frisian (spoken by a small number of people in Friesland, which is a province in the northern Netherlands, and in certain adjoining islands). Though none of these lists would be identical, the words would obviously be closely related.

The languages we have named are all members of the Germanic branch (sometimes called the *Teutonic* branch) of the Indo-European family, and may be considered siblings. The following diagram[1] groups the languages more systematically:

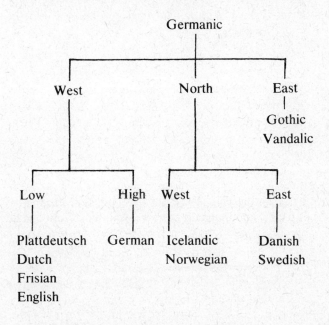

---

[1]Based on Stuart Robertson and Frederic G. Cassidy, *The Development of Modern English*, 2nd ed., New York: Prentice Hall, Inc., 1954, p. 33.

► If you or any of your relatives or friends happen to know Swedish, Norwegian, Plattdeutsch, or Yiddish, write in that language the numbers from one to ten and the words for *mother, father, brother, sister, widow, wolf, snow,* and *head*

► Draw a map of Europe to show where speakers of the various modern Germanic languages now live. Your map should show the homes of English, German, Plattdeutsch, Icelandic, Norwegian, Danish, Swedish, Dutch, Flemish, and Frisian.

Gothic was the language of the Goths, who overran the Roman Empire in its declining years. Only a few fragments of its written language remain. It is an extinct, or "dead," language. Languages, like people, are born, grow, and eventually die, though the birth and usually the death of a language cannot be dated precisely. Vandalic, closely related to Gothic, was spoken by the Vandals, who once terrorized much of western Europe; it too is now a dead language.

All the languages shown in the diagram are siblings, but some are closer than others, just as in a large family some brothers and sisters associate more closely with one another. We could say, for example, that Icelandic and Norwegian are nonidentical twins, as are Danish and Swedish. Most closely akin to English are Frisian, Dutch, and Plattdeutsch, with

High German (the standard literary German) not far removed.[2]

Let's look now at some other words from some of the Germanic languages to see whether the similarities are confined to numbers. Sometimes the relationships will be more easily visible if we use older forms.

English:	mother	father	brother	sister
Old English:	mōdor	fæder[5]	brōþor	sweostor
Old Norse:	mōðir[3]	faðir	broðir	systir
Gothic:	_____[4]	fadar	broþar	swistar
German:	Mutter	Vater	Bruder	Schwester

English:	widow	wolf	snow	head
Old English:	widuwe	wulf	snāw	hēafod
Old Norse:	_____	ulfr	snær	haufoð
Gothic:	widuwo	wulfs	snaiws	haubiþ
German:	Wittwe	Wolf	Schnee	Haupt

These lists could go on and on, with examples from all of the Germanic languages. Longer lists would make it possible to see also that where differences

---

[2]Yiddish is in a sense a child of High German. It is based on several Middle High German dialects, mixed with Hebrew and Slavic words, and written in Hebrew letters. It is spoken chiefly by Jews in places east of Germany, including parts of the Soviet Union, but also exists in the United States and many other countries. Similarly, Afrikaans (pronounced "af-ruh-kahns") may be considered a child of Dutch. It is spoken in South Africa and was developed from the Dutch of seventeenth-century settlers. Flemish, spoken mainly in parts of Belgium, is a blend of Dutch dialects. One of three official languages of Luxembourg, called Luxembourgian or Letzeburgesch, is a blend of Germanic dialects. Pidgin English, spoken especially in many Pacific areas, may be regarded as a child of English.

[3]Both þ (called "thorn") and ð (called "eth") represent the sounds of *th*.
[4]A blank indicates either that the form of the word is unknown or that the word came from a non-Germanic source.
[5]The sound of æ was about like that of *a* in *bat*.

between forms of words exist in two of the languages, there is often a pattern in the differences. For example, Old English *mōdor* and *fæder* both have *d*'s, while the corresponding German *Mutter* and *Vater* use the unvoiced sound of *t*, but the *th* sound in Old English *brōþor* corresponds to the *d* sound of German *Bruder*.

It should not be concluded, however, that *all* words in the Germanic languages are related. For instance, English uses *lard* to refer to the fat of a pig, but German uses the completely different *Schweine-fett* (literally "swine fat"). The explanation is that English borrowed *lard* from an Old French word derived from Latin, but German kept the Germanic compound.

The siblinghood of the Germanic languages is most clearly revealed through the existence of obviously related words like *mother* and *Mutter* or *father* and *Vater*. (Such pairs of words, which are derived from the same older word, are called cognates.) However, there is plenty of other evidence, which can be summarized briefly.

For one thing, the Germanic languages all have rather few verb forms. Modern English *carry*, for example, has only the forms *carry, carries, carried,* and *carrying,* which can be expanded by the use of such auxiliaries as *is, has, have, will, may, must, do, did,* and *should* (*is carrying, has carried, will carry, may have carried,* etc.). But if you were to look at a full conjugation of the same verb in some non-Germanic languages, you might find that it occupies two or more pages, with many different forms of the verb. The Latin *portāre* (to carry), for example, has forms ranging from simple *portō* (I carry) to *portā-*

bimus (we shall carry), *portāverunt* (they carried), or *portāveritis* (you will have carried).

A second characteristic is that the Germanic languages all have—or once did have—what have been called "strong" and "weak" declensions of adjectives. When a German uses *der, die,* or *das* before an adjective and a noun subject, the adjective ends in *-e: der kleine Bruder* means "the little brother." But when the German uses what is called an "*ein* word" before an adjective and a noun subject, the adjective ends in *-er* for a masculine noun, *-e* for a feminine noun, and *-es* for a neuter noun: *ein kleiner Bruder* means "a little brother." Old English once treated adjectives similarly, but the distinctions have been lost in Modern English—to no one's regret.

A third difference is that Germanic languages tend to keep the accent or stress on the same syllable in different forms of a word (unless the word is borrowed from some other language). For example, *lóve, lóving, lóver,* and *belóved* all accent the root syllable *lóv-*. In contrast, note the shift of accent in the present tense of the Latin word for *love: ámō, ámās, ámāt, amāmus, amātis, ámant.*

A fourth major difference between the Germanic languages and the other languages of the Indo-European family results from the fact that in the process of becoming Germanic (several thousand years ago), many of the Indo-European consonants changed to other sounds. There is an interesting story about how scholars found out about these "shifts."

A Danish linguist, Rasmus Rask (1787–1832), wrote grammars of Icelandic, Old Norse, Old English, Spanish, Frisian, and Italian, and was familiar with a number of other languages. His studies began to show him that words in the Germanic languages were often like words in some of the other languages, except for certain regular differences in consonants. For example, English *three* and *thou* seemed related to Latin *trēs* and French *tu,* and other English words with *th* were similar to the corresponding Latin and French (or Spanish, Italian, Portuguese, Romanian, or even Celtic and Russian) words. Rask found many such examples—not just with *th* and *t*—and concluded, in 1818, that they had come about because for some reason various consonants had changed their sounds in Germanic, but not in the other languages of the family. But Rask was busy with other things and didn't do much to publicize his discovery.

Now a German, Jacob Grimm (1785–1863), enters the story. (He and his brother Wilhelm were both interested in folklore and a few years before had published a children's book that we still call *Grimm's Fairy Tales.*) In 1819 Jacob had brought out a German grammar, and before the second edition in 1822 he had found out about Rask's work, which greatly impressed him. He set to work finding still more examples of the sound shifts and showing just how regular they were. He wrote up the results in the second edition of his grammar. This is why linguists now talk of "Grimm's Law" when discussing the shifts, even though "Rask's Law" would be a more accurate name.

Here are a few examples of Grimm's Law. Remember that it is *sounds* we are considering—not letters.

Indo-European	*Germanic*	*Examples*
/b/ ⟶	/p/	*Latin* labium, *English* lip; *Lithuanian* dubùs, *English* deep

8

[This means that the sound /b/, which remained in other Indo-European languages, shifted to the sound /p/ in Germanic languages.]

/d/ ⟶ /t/	*Latin* **d**uo, *Dutch* **tw**ee; *Greek* **d**rys, *English* **t**ree	
/g/ ⟶ /k/	*Latin* **a**ger (field), *English* a**c**re; *Latin* **g**enus, *English* **k**in	
/p/ ⟶ /f/	*Latin* **p**iscis, *English* **f**ish; *Latin* **p**ater, *English* **f**ather	
/t/ ⟶ /th/	*Latin* **t**rēs, *English* **th**ree; *Polish* **t**arn, *English* **th**orn	
/k/ ⟶ /h/	*Latin* **c**ornū, *English* **h**orn; *Latin* **c**ordis, *German* **H**erz (heart)	
/bh/ ⟶ /b/	*Sanskrit* **bh**rātār, *German* **B**ruder	
/dh/ ⟶ /d/	*Sanskrit* ma**dh**u, *English* mea**d**	
/gh/ ⟶ /g/	*Indo-European* ***gh**ostis,[6] *English* **g**uest	

[The Indo-European /bh/, /dh/, and /gh/ were pronounced something like "buh-huh," "duh-huh," and "guh-huh."]

It is not necessary to memorize these consonant changes, but knowing about them may sometimes reveal not only the brotherhood of Germanic languages but also unsuspected cousinship with other languages.

► If you know French, Spanish, Italian, Portuguese, Latin, or Russian, compare one English verb with the

[6]Since there are no written records of Indo-European, this form is "reconstructed" on the basis of available evidence, somewhat as a dinosaur's skeleton can be reconstructed on the basis of a few bones. The asterisk is a symbol used by linguists to indicate that the form is a reconstruction.

corresponding verb in that language, in order to show the smaller number of distinctive verb forms in English. (See page 6.) Perhaps you have or can get a grammar book of the foreign language to show the full conjugation.

▶ The following is a fairly difficult exercise, but it may be fun if you like to play detective. Look again at the list of Germanic consonant changes, pages 8–9. You can see, for example, that a Germanic word containing the sound /p/ is likely to have a related word with the sound /b/ in Latin or Greek or some other non-Germanic Indo-European language. Thus English *lip* has the Latin relative *labium*.

a. What sound is likely to be in Latin, Greek, Sanskrit, etc., corresponding to the boldfaced part of the following words (and the thorn and the eth in the last two)? You will need to work backward from the list of consonant shifts, since the sounds represented below show the results after the shifts.

through	**sh**ape	**h**ome
foul	**t**each	**th**reat
cool	**b**e	**th**ink
timber	**f**ood	stam**p**
few	**t**o	**þ**olian
thumb	**t**ug	(OE for "tolerate")
hall	**c**arve	mor**ð**or
a**ch**e	**f**eather	(OE for "murder")

b. The following list consists of words from non-Germanic languages. Each word is related to one of those in *a*. Try to decide which word corresponds to which. Do as many as you can without using the clues supplied. (The meanings are sometimes the same, but not always.) In this exercise, usually the endings of the foreign words may be ignored.

Latin *paucus* (not many)
  (Our word *paucity* comes from it.)
Latin *trans* (as in our *transcontinental*)
Latin *cella* (hut)
  (The *l*'s did not change.)
Sanskrit *bheu*
  (This is related to a very common one-syllable English verb.)
Greek *pteron* (wing)
  (A pterodactyl could fly.)
Latin *mortis* (death)
Latin *ducere* (to lead)
  (Look for two consonant shifts in this word.)
Latin *dicere* (to say)
Latin *tumere* (to swell)
Greek *stembein*
  (The English noun names something you use frequently.)
Latin *trudere* (to push)
  (Look for two consonant shifts in this word.)
Latin *tongere* (to know)
  (Again, two consonant shifts.)
Latin *domus* (house)
  (What may a house be built of?)
Greek *graphein* (to write)
  (Think of an old method of writing.)
Latin *panis* (bread)
Lithuanian *kёmas* (village)
Russian *do* (up to)

Latin *puter* (rotten)
   (Our word *putrid* comes from it.)
Greek *agōnia* (struggle)
   (A struggle may be painful.)
Latin *tollere* (to bear)
Latin *scabere* (to form by scraping)
Latin *gelu* (frost)
   (It's cold, isn't it?)

2. Cousins
of the English Language

The exercise you have just done on consonant shifts would not have been possible with such languages as Chinese or Arabic or any of the American Indian languages. Any similarities between those languages and Germanic languages are due only to chance or, occasionally, to borrowing.

The world has several hundred families of languages besides Indo-European, although some of them are very small. The American Indian languages are divided into half a dozen superfamilies and a large number of families. Indo-Chinese includes the languages of China, Tibet, and Indochina. Japanese is a quite different language from Chinese, and Korean is different from both. Dravidian languages are spoken extensively in southern India. Malay-Polynesian languages are scattered through the islands of the Pacific and the Indian Ocean. Semitic languages include Hebrew, Arabic, Ethiopic, and others. Hamitic languages consist of Egyptian, the Berber dialects of northern Africa, and others. South of the Sahara are a large number of language families, sometimes grouped as Sudanese, Bantu, and Hottentot and Bushman.

None of these language families has any apparent relationship to Indo-European, the family to which Germanic belongs. In this section, we'll concentrate on the other Indo-European languages, which we call cousins of Germanic.

The following diagram[7] summarizes what we will look at in more detail:

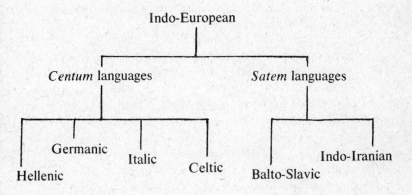

Why are the languages called "centum" and "satem"? Well, in Latin the word for *hundred* is *centum*, which is pronounced with a *k* sound. In Avestan, a form of Old Persian, the word is *satem*, with an *s* sound. This difference in pronunciation, which was paralleled in many other words, helps to distinguish the *centum* group of languages from the *satem* group. The groups could just as well be called

[7]Based on Thomas Pyles, *The Origins and Development of the English Language,* New York: Harcourt Brace Jovanovich, 1964, pp. 80–81.

"the *k*-sound languages" and "the *s*-sound languages."
(There are, of course, many other differences between
the two groups.) In Germanic languages the *k* sound
became an *h* sound, as Grimm's Law points out. So
hundred, *centum*, and *satem*, despite their differences
in form and pronunciation, are historically the same
word.

The Hellenic cousins of English include the
ancient Greek dialects used by Homer, Sophocles,
Plato, and other famous Greek authors, and modern
Greek.

The Italic branch consists of the languages spoken
in ancient Roman times—chiefly Latin, but also Oscan
and Umbrian—and the modern descendants of Latin:
Spanish, Portuguese, Romanian, French, and Italian.

The Celtic languages were once widely spoken in
the British Isles; they still survive, especially in parts
of Ireland, Scotland, and Wales. A diagram of this
branch looks like this:

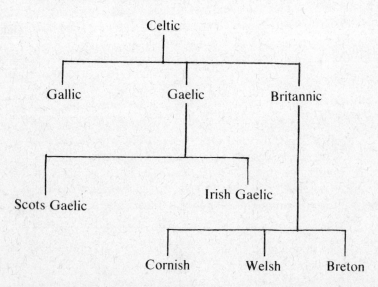

In the *satem* group, linguists often include as separate branches Armenian and Albanian, though these are not on the chart on page 13. Armenian is a language of Asia Minor and the Caucasus, and Albanian is spoken in Albania and parts of southern Italy.

The Balto-Slavic branch has Russian as its major member but includes other important languages, as this diagram, based on Thomas Pyles, shows:

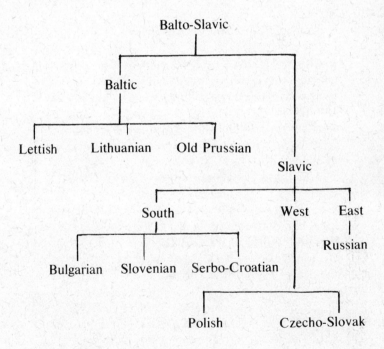

The Indo-Iranian branch has many millions of users of its languages, which are charted in simple form by Pyles. (See page 16.)

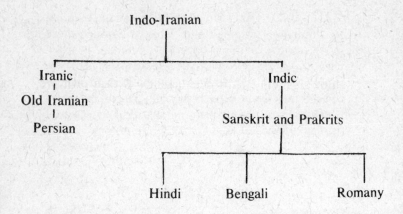

```
                    Indo-Iranian
                         |
        ┌────────────────┴────────────────┐
     Iranic                             Indic
        |                                 |
   Old Iranian                   Sanskrit and Prakrits
        |                                 |
     Persian            ┌─────────────────┼─────────────────┐
                        |                 |                 |
                      Hindi            Bengali            Romany
```

Remembering that *Iran* is the modern name for Persia will help to explain the words *Iranian* and *Iranic*. The Indic branch includes not only some of the languages of India but also some of the languages of the independent nations Pakistan, Nepal, and Ceylon. Sanskrit is dead as a spoken language, though once used by scores of millions. The name *Prakrits* refers to the ancient Indic languages other than Sanskrit, and sometimes to the modern ones as well. Hindi is the leading language of present-day India, and Bengali is spoken in northeast India and eastern Pakistan. Romany has nothing to do with Rome; it is the language of the Gypsies, who have roved about the globe for centuries and whose origin was in the Indian peninsula.

If we could assemble fifty or a hundred people, all of whom were first or second or third cousins, we would expect that they would be more alike than a randomly chosen group of people. Most of them, for instance, would probably have eyes and hair of the same color, or be taller or shorter than the human average, or be alike in some other ways, even though their differences from one another would also be great.

It is much the same with language cousins. Although all of them have individual qualities of their own, we expect language cousins to be alike in some ways.

The Indo-European cousins are alike, first, in having basically the same words for certain things—a common word-stock, as it is called. This does not mean that *most* of their words are the same, but only that many of their fairly common words obviously have the same ancestry.

Earlier we looked at some words common to the Germanic languages. Now we'll look at a few words in some other Indo-European languages and see whether we can note any family resemblances:

English:	three	seven	mother	brother	me
Latin:	trēs	septem	mater	frater	me
Greek:	treis	hepta	meter	phrātēr	me
Celtic:	tri	secht	mathair	brathair	me
Lithuanian:	tri	septyni	moter	brolis	manen
Sanskrit:	tri	sapta	matar	bhrātār	me

The English word *night* is *Nacht* in German, and *Nacht* has a cousinly resemblance to Latin *noctis*, Greek *nuktós*, Spanish *noche*, Italian *notte*, and less obviously to French *nuit*.

Honey and a drink made from honey have names that go back to Indo-European *melit* and *medhu*:

The former appears, for example, in Greek *méli* (honey) and *mélissa* (bee), Latin *mel* (honey), and Old English *milisc* (honey-sweet) and *mildēaw* (mildew—literally, "honey-dew"). The latter appears, among many other places, in Sanskrit *madhu* (honey, mead), Greek *méthu* (intoxicating drink), Dutch *mede* (mead), and Old English *medu* (mead).[8]

Among other common words in the Indo-European word-stock are those for *winter, spring, snow, dog, horse, cow, sheep, bear, oak, willow,* and *pine.*

As a final example of the cousinship in vocabulary, let's do a little more counting. The words in the last column below are from Japanese, which is not an Indo-European language, and do not look at all like the others. In the other columns, the similarities among the cousins should be apparent, though less so than in the Germanic languages, as you can see in the chart on page 5.

English	Latin	Greek	Russian
one	ūnus	heis	odin
two	duo	duo	dva
three	trēs	treis	tri
four	quattuor	tettares	chetyre
five	quinque	pente	pyat'
six	sex	hex	shest'
seven	septem	hepta	sem'
eight	octō	oktō	vosem'
nine	novem	ennea	devyat'
ten	decem	deka	desyat'
. . .			
hundred	centum	hekaton	sto

[8]Robertson and Cassidy, *op. cit.,* pp. 19–20.

Many more examples could be given that would confirm the conclusion that, despite differences in form, many words in the various languages of the Indo-European family come from the same original source.

A second way in which the Indo-European languages are alike is that they use inflections to show such things as plural number or a past tense. An inflection is usually an added ending (a suffix), but it may be a prefix or an internal change. For example, in English we say *one street* but *two streets;* the *-s* is an inflection to show plurality. Or we say *I shout* but *yesterday I shouted;* the *-ed* is an indicator of past tense. If we say *they buy* and *they bought,* the internal change in *bought* is also an inflection to show past tense. Old English had an inflectional prefix *ge-* (as

Polish	*Hindustani*	*Japanese*
jeden	ek	ichi
dwa	do	ni
trzy	tin	san
cztery	char	shi
pięć	panch	go
sześć	chha	roku
siedem	sat	shichi
osiem	ath	hachi
dziewięć	nau	ku
dziesięć	das	ju
sto	sau	hyaku

German still has), which appeared in many verbs as a sign of a past participle.

Other Indo-European languages make even more use of inflections than Modern English does. (Old English, as will be seen later, was much more heavily inflected than the English of today.) A Latin verb, as we illustrated on pages 6–7, may have a few dozen inflectional endings; Latin nouns used different endings not only for singular and plural, but also to show whether the noun was the subject, the object, the indirect object, an object of certain prepositions, a possessive, or a vocative (the form used in addressing a person). Adjectives also changed their endings to agree with their nouns.

Sanskrit, Russian, Welsh, Armenian—in fact, all the first, second, third, and umpteenth cousins of the Germanic languages—made or make great use of inflections.

In contrast, some of the world's languages other than Indo-European use no inflections or very few. Chinese is the best example of a virtually uninflected language. Its words are nearly all single syllables, and inflected forms like our *churches* or *longer* do not exist; separate words do the job done by our *-es, -er, -ed,* and other inflectional endings. In addition, in spoken Chinese, tone and stress may affect both meaning and grammatical use. Thus *t'ang* in a high tone means "soup," but in other tones it means "sugar," "lie down," or "hot." (The story is told of a high American official who tried to say in Vietnamese, a language something like Chinese, "Long live Vietnam." Because his tones were wrong, what he really said was "The ducks are wet.")

At the opposite end from monosyllabic languages like Chinese are "incorporating" languages in which the important parts of a sentence are incorporated into a single "word." Many of the languages of American Indians were of this type. Algeo and Pyles give this analysis[9] of an example from Eskimo:

Qasuiirsarvigssarsingitluinarnarpuq
'Someone did not at all find a suitable resting place.'

Qasu /-iir /-sar /-vig /
tired / *not* / *causing to be* / *place for* /

-ssar /-si /
suitable / *find* /

-ngit /-luinar /-nar /
not / *completely* / *someone* /

-puq
third person singular indicative mood

Still other languages are of a type called "agglutinative." They make use of prefixes and suffixes, as inflected languages do, only more so. Often they attach two, three, or more affixes to the same word. Each of these affixes has a single definite meaning, in contrast to an inflectional ending like the *-o* in the Latin verb *portō,* which signifies several things: first person, singular number, present tense, active voice, and indicative mood. An example of agglutination is the Chinook Indian word *ačimlúda,* in which *a* signifies future time, *č* means "he," *i* means "it," *m* means "thee," *l* means "to," *úd* means "give," and *a* again

[9]John Algeo and Thomas Pyles, *Problems in the Origin and Development of the English Language,* New York: Harcourt Brace Jovanovich, 1966, p. 75.

shows future time. Put them all together and you come out with "He will give it to thee."

Other languages, then, differ from Indo-European in two major ways. One is that they do not share in the common word-stock of Indo-European (except for an occasional borrowing). The other is that they ordinarily do not use as many inflections as the Indo-European languages do, or do not use them in the same ways.

▶ On a globe, point to the general area of the homelands of these Indo-European languages: English, German, the Scandinavian languages, French, Spanish, Portuguese, Italian, Welsh, Scots Gaelic, Irish Gaelic, Albanian, Armenian, Lithuanian, Bulgarian, Russian, Polish, Czecho-Slovak, Persian, Hindi, Bengali. Or draw a map (or maps) of the world and show the approximate locations of these places, some of which may overlap.

▶ Explain in your own words the basis for the division into *centum* and *satem* languages.

▶ If you know an Indo-European language that is not Germanic, prepare a brief report on one way in which that language is similar to English. You may want to give examples of similar words (cognates), or discuss word order, or describe the inflectional system, or something else.

► Here is a list of famous authors. Using a dictionary or an encyclopedia when necessary, indicate which of the Indo-European languages was used by each.

Jonas Basanavičius
Karel Čapek
Miguel de Cervantes
Dafydd ap Gwilym
  (Look in *D*'s.)
Gabriele D'Annunzio
Euripides
Firdausi
Almeida-Garrett

Johann W. von Goethe
Victor Hugo
Henrik Ibsen
Adam Mickiewicz
John Milton
Leo Tolstoy
Tulsī Dās
  (Look in *T*'s.)
Vergil

► If you are fortunate enough to know a language that is not in the Indo-European family, prepare a report on any differences (other than vocabulary) that you can think of. For example, if you know Chinese, you may elaborate on the brief description given on page 20.

3. The Ancestors of English

Since the early Indo-Europeans could not write, we have no historical records of them and their wanderings. We do not know for sure who they were or even whether they were European or Asiatic or a mixture of both. However, scholars have painstakingly pieced together bits of evidence that allow us to draw a few conclusions. Let's look at some of them.

The common word-stock of the Indo-European languages provides most of the evidence:

    a. There are no common names for tropical trees or plants, but there are common ones for vegetation of the temperate zone.

    b. Similarly, there are no common words for crocodiles, hippopotamuses, elephants, lions, tigers, or raccoons, but there are common words for wolves, bears, hares, and beavers.

    c. There are common words for winter and snow, but not, for example, for monsoon or jungle.

    d. There seems to be no common word for ocean.

    e. There are common words for certain domestic animals: dogs, pigs, horses, cows, sheep—but not for donkeys and goats and camels.

    f. There are common words for honey and a drink made from honey.

    g. According to Professor H. H. Bender, whose *Home of the Indo-Europeans* is the most thorough examination of the subject, the Lithuanian people have lived in about the same locality for five thousand years or more (the duration of the Indo-European period), and their language still retains more Indo-European characteristics than any other does.[10]

On the basis of such evidence, the following conclusions appear justified:

    a. The early Indo-European home was in a temperate rather than a tropical area.

[10]H. H. Bender, *The Home of the Indo-Europeans,* Princeton: Princeton University Press, 1922, p. 20.

b. The home was probably not on a seacoast.
c. The early Indo-Europeans apparently farmed or at least kept grazing animals; unless they patronized wild bees only, they may have been settled enough to maintain apiaries.
d. Lithuania (now one of the republics of the Soviet Union, in the western part of Russia, on the Baltic Sea) is the most likely early home, although it is possible that the site was across the Urals in Asia.

Over a period of many centuries, from wherever the original home was, the Indo-Europeans spread out and prospered. They must have been warriors as well as farmers, since they very likely encountered a great deal of opposition as they moved into territory new to them. Records of their countless raids and battles and wars, though, do not exist.

They spread westward, eventually conquering and settling almost all of Europe. With few exceptions, the languages of Europe are Indo-European. One exception is Finnish, or Finno-Ugrian, a language that belongs to a family called Ural-Altaic. Eight varieties of Finnish are spoken by the Finns, Lapps, Estonians, and others. These northern European people apparently resisted conquest by the powerful Indo-European soldiers.

The Hungarians, too, resisted enough to avoid absorption. The Hungarian language is also Ural-Altaic, though it is not very similar to Finnish.

In the foothills of the Pyrenees, partly in France and partly in Spain, is another population island that long resisted conquest. This is the land of the proud Basques, with a total population of less than two million, most of whom live on the Spanish side of the line. The Basque language, which apparently originated in Asia Minor, is gradually dying out as more and more Basques conduct their affairs in Spanish or French. Thus even today the Indo-European conquest goes on.

Southward, other Indo-Europeans marched far and settled in various places all the way down to India. The Slavic people and the Greeks, as we have seen, are Indo-Europeans, but the Turks are not. The distant reaches of Russia represent partly Indo-European ancestry, partly Mongolian and other Asiatic heritage. Iran (Persia), as we have noted, is Indo-European in language. And still farther southeast, the vast subcontinent of India reflects in its languages the extensive spread, conquest, settlement, and influence of the Indo-Europeans.

When invaders conquer a land and remain in it as permanent residents, they do business and intermarry with the surviving natives, who learn parts of the invaders' language and teach the invaders parts of their own language. Thus both languages change greatly over a period of time and generally merge into a single language.

The Indo-Europeans who settled in what we call northern Germany and Scandinavia thus found their language developing in one way. Those who settled in southern Europe, since they were mingling with different peoples, found that their language developed differently. So Old Norse is quite different from Latin, even though both languages are Indo-European.

Similarly, in the Slavic areas and in Greece and Iran and India, the original Indo-European changed greatly. The basic grammar was still Indo-European, and the languages still clung to some of the same words (though often with considerably different pronunciations), but after a few centuries an Indo-European from Greece could not understand one from Russia or Iran or India or even from Italy or Germany.

We do not know just what kind of people these Indo-Europeans encountered when they moved into northwestern Europe and the British Isles, but there is evidence from archaeology that the inhabitants of the British Isles had come much earlier from the Mediterranean area and from Africa and Asia. They had long skulls, they made weapons and tools of flint, and they were an agricultural people who raised cattle, sheep, goats, and dogs.

At a time believed to be between 2000 and 1400 B.C. these people were conquered by round-headed men who may have been among the waves of Indo-Europeans. These conquerors had advanced to the stage of using bronze, an alloy made of tin and copper. Cornwall, in southern England, was valuable to them because of its rich tin deposits. With their bronze tools they could clear the forests and till the soil. They were good enough engineers that they could haul many miles the huge stones still standing at Stonehenge—a monumental ruin that may have served as a gigantic astronomical calendar.

The Indo-European invaders of the British Isles and northwestern Europe, like those who went in other directions, killed some of the natives, married some of the native women, and gradually merged with the people who had preceded them. The languages also merged, but they were not identical throughout the regions because the earlier settlers had come from different places and had spoken different languages. Besides, Indo-European itself had no doubt broken up into various dialects and even different languages before some of the conquests occurred.

With the countless waves of migration and conquest, northern and western Europe—indeed, almost all of Europe—became a huge melting pot. The tall and the short, the dark and the light, the brown-eyed and the blue-eyed, the culturally advanced and the culturally retarded, and those whose ancestors had come from Europe and Asia and Africa—all intermingled for centuries.

Out of some of this mingling came the various Germanic peoples and Germanic languages, one of which is English. In the next chapter we'll trace the further mingling that took place in England during the centuries we have historical records for.

▶ Summarize the evidence presented above concerning the original home of the Indo-Europeans.

▶ Assume that Lithuania is the original home of Indo-European. Find Lithuania on a map of Europe. Trace some of the possible paths from there which the early Indo-Europeans and their descendants throughout the centuries may have followed as they moved west, east, and south (as far as India). What natural barriers, such as mountain chains, would they have encountered? Why were China, Japan, and much of central Asia apparently not touched by the Indo-Europeans?

▶ Imagine that you are living in prehistoric times. You are a member of an army that has conquered territory new to you. You see a pretty native girl and want to make her your wife, but since her language is different, you cannot talk with her. How do you court her? After your marriage, how do you converse? How do you talk with your native neighbors? What language will your children learn? In a few generations, what will the language of your descendants be like?

2

"the
true-BORN
englishman"

King William III of England, also called William of Orange, was criticized because he was Dutch rather than English. In 1701 Daniel Defoe, best known today as the author of *Robinson Crusoe*, rose to William's defense with a long poem called "The True-Born Englishman."

The main point made by Defoe in this satirical poem was that there was no such thing as an Englishman, for the English people were an amalgam of tribes and nations:

Go back to elder times and ages past,
And nations into long oblivion cast;
To old Britannia's youthful days retire,
And there for true-born Englishmen inquire.
Britannia freely will disown the name,
And hardly knows herself from whence they came.

Defoe claimed that early England "by sev'ral crowds of wand'ring thieves [was] o'errun," and summarized in the following lines the history from the time of Julius Caesar (100? to 44 B.C.) to the conquest by William the Conqueror (1066 A.D.):

The Romans first with Julius Caesar came,
Including all the nations of that name,
Gauls, Greeks, and Lombards, and, by computation,
Auxiliaries or slaves of ev'ry nation.
With Hengist, Saxons; Danes with Sueno came,
In search of plunder, not in search of fame.
Scots, Picts, and Irish from the Hibernian shore,
And conq'ring William brought the Normans o'er.

Defoe refers to the language as "Your Roman-Saxon-Danish-Norman English." He points out further additions to the British ancestry:

Dutch, Walloons, Flemings, Irishmen, and Scots,
Vaudois and Valtelins, and Huguenots,
In good Queen Bess's charitable reign,
Supplied us with three hundred thousand men.

Moreover, says Defoe, King Charles II in the seventeenth century brought in "foreign courtiers," "French cooks," and a number of other people that Defoe considered undesirable.

Fate jumbled them together, God knows how;
Whate'er they were, they're true-born English now.
A true-born Englishman's a contradiction,
In speech an irony, in fact a fiction; . . .
A metaphor invented to express
A man akin to all the universe.

Although Defoe's history is not completely accurate, his point is valid that the English of his day were a mixture of peoples. They still are, only more so. In this chapter, we'll explore some details of the mixture and note how the mixing influenced the language.

1. The Celts and the Romans

The Celts (pronounced either "keltz" or "seltz"), a people who spoke an Indo-European language, conquered most of the British Isles before the dawn of written history. They were probably the "round-heads" mentioned in the first chapter, who used bronze tools and weapons and who overcame the "long-skulled" inhabitants. These long-skulls were probably the Picts, whose language may or may not have been Indo-European. They were pushed into the far corners of the islands but continued for many centuries to harass the Celts.

The Celts occupied most of the British Isles at the time when the Angles and Saxons came over (the fifth and sixth centuries A.D.). One would expect that, because there were so many Celts, many of their words would have been taken over by the Angles and Saxons and would have survived in the language. But this was not the case. Except for place-names, the Celts contributed few words that are now in the English vocabulary. Among the small number surviving from this early period are *combe* (a narrow valley), *tor* (a hill), *binn* (a bin), and *bannock* (a griddle cake). About a thousand years later, however, English borrowed from the Irish and Scottish descendants of the Celts some additional words such as *blarney, brogue, colleen, crag, galore, leprechaun, plaid, shamrock, shillelagh,* and *slogan.*

Place-names from early Celtic were much more numerous. P. H. Reaney, in his authoritative book *The Origin of English Place-Names,* devotes a 27-page chapter to "The Celtic Element." Often the modern spelling is quite different from the old. Thus Celtic *Eboràcon* or *Ebrauc* through a series of changes became modern *York* (which also survives in the American *New York, Yorktown,* etc.). *London* appears to be derived from a Celtic **londo-* (wild, bold); the Romans recorded the name as *Londinium.* The names of many British rivers, including *Thames, Trent, Avon,* and *Dee,* are Celtic in origin. So are the names of some of the shires (counties), such as *Devon, Cornwall, Berkshire,* and the Isle of *Wight.*

Some of the British compound place-names, which Americans find so fascinating, date back at least in part to Celtic sources. For example, there was in Celtic times a large forest, called *Lyme* (elm), in Lancashire and Cheshire. A place near the south edge of that area is still called *Ashton-under-Lyme,* and related place-names include *Lyme Wood, Lime-hurst,* and *Lyme Park.*

In 55 and 54 B.C. Julius Caesar came from Rome, made a partial conquest of the Celts, and tried to exact tribute from them. A few years later, Roman legions crossed the Strait of Dover in greater numbers and began a conquest that was to take over a century to complete. By about 100 A.D. the Celts, like the earlier Picts, had been pushed in great numbers to the outer edges of the islands (now Wales, Ireland, and Scotland) or across the channel to Brittany. Roman Britain was then a reality.

The Romans built roads, forts, walls, and large military camps. The remains of some of these still exist today; in places we may still walk about in remarkably sturdy and well-preserved stone fortresses that were built to protect the Roman soldiers from the vengeful Celts.

Although the Romans remained in Britain for several centuries, only a few words that they brought in during the period were destined to find their way into what would later be the English language, mainly because the Romans and the Celts mingled very little. However, the Roman paved roads were called *strata via*, which became Old English *strǣt*, Modern English *street*. Roman camps were called *castra*, which was Anglicized to *caster, cester,* or *chester* and survives in many place-names like *Leicester, Lancaster, Rochester,* and *Chester*. Latin *vallum* is the ancestor of our *wall, furca* gave us *fork,* and *monachus* is the ancestor of *monk*.

As the Roman Empire declined and was itself partly overrun by invaders, the Roman legions withdrew from Britain to protect their own homeland. If they had remained, we would probably today be speaking an Italic language something like French or Spanish or Italian. But the fate known as history decreed otherwise. The Romans left by 410 A.D., and the Celts moved back to the land from which their ancestors had been driven, fighting often among themselves and fighting also against the Picts, who through all these centuries had continued to cling stubbornly to the edges of the islands. Not until the ninth century were the Picts absorbed by the Scots, who were originally an Irish group that had become separated from the other Celts.

► Little is known about the Picts, not even for sure whether they were Indo-European. Using whatever reference books are available, write a paragraph summarizing what is known or believed to be true.

► Referring to an encyclopedia or a book on English history, write a paragraph or two about the Roman conquest of Britain.

► Why, in your opinion, did words like *street, wall,* and *-chester* (or a variant) survive from the Roman conquest, but not words for Roman political institutions or military units?

► Besides the examples given on page 35, list as many other place-names derived from *castra* as you can think of.

► In an encyclopedia or a history of the Roman Empire, find out exactly what was happening to Rome that caused her to withdraw her forces from Britain.

2. The Angles, Saxons, and Jutes

When the Roman legions left, the Celts found that they could not cope with the warlike Picts and Scots. They begged the Romans to return, but a single legion of Roman soldiers—all that could be spared—helped very little. So the Celts sent a call to "parts across the sea" (as the Venerable Bede, the ancient historian, put it), asking various Germanic leaders in northern Europe to come to their aid.

The first answer to their appeal came in 449 A.D., in the form of a small group of soldiers led by two Jutish brothers, Hengist and Horsa; shiploads of other Germanic fighters followed over a period of many years. These adventurers from the north were successful in driving back the Picts and the Scots for the Britons, but then instead of leaving, many of them decided to stay on and take over the country for themselves. For the next century and a half, more and more of these men arrived from the north to settle in Britain. Sometimes they allowed the Celts to remain; more often they pushed them back toward the western and northern parts of the islands or even across the English Channel to the part of France called Brittany (French *Bretagne*) in their honor. And so, ironically, the help the Celts themselves had sought proved, in the end, to be their undoing.

Most historians say that these Germanic people were of three major tribes, plus a scattering of others. They were Jutes, Saxons, and Angles, arriving in that order probably. The Jutes, it is thought, came from the northern section of the Jutland Peninsula, the section that is now the Continental part of Denmark. Saxony, from which most of the Saxons probably came, was a ten thousand square mile area of northern Germany, near the mouth of the Elbe River. Schleswig, in northwest Germany, was the home of the Angles.

The Jutes settled in the southeastern part of Britain, the Saxons in the rest of the south, and the Angles in the much larger area north of the Thames to the Scottish Highlands. Many of the differences in Modern English dialects can be explained by these differences in settlements, since Jutish, Saxon, and Anglian were themselves somewhat different Germanic dialects.

The conquests and settlements by the Germanic tribes from the north—the Jutes, the Saxons, the Angles—were among the most important events in British history and had far-reaching effects, as you will see. It is interesting to note that though the Angles were the last of the three to arrive, they were the most dominant. They were so influential, in fact, that their name—*Anglisc* or *Englisc*—was used to refer to all the northern invaders. This is how the country came to be called *Englaland* and then *England* (the "land of the Angles") and the language *English*.

In the next chapter, we'll look closely at the Germanic language used by these settlers from the Continent. Now, however, let's see what else of linguistic importance happened to the English before 1066.

In the sixth and seventh centuries the Romans tried a different kind of invasion. This was a peaceful one, conducted by missionary priests bent on Christianizing the pagan inhabitants. The priests succeeded, and England has been a Christian nation since that time (though no longer predominantly Catholic),

The English adopted various Latin words from the priests and monks. As is to be expected, some of these were church words. You should be able to guess the Modern English forms of Latin *apostolus*, *diaconus*, *daemon*, and *hymnus*. Latin *papa* is the ancestor of *pope*, and Latin *schola* gave us *school*, *scholar*, and related words.

Indirectly, the Greek language contributed to English at this time and later. Latin had borrowed from Greek the six words just listed, as well as its words for *alms*, *martyr*, *bishop*, *psalm*, *devil*, and others. These Greek words, then, entered English by way of Latin.

► Here are some Latin words that were borrowed in the seventh century or earlier. See if you can guess the Modern English forms. Some clues have been provided.

pirum (a fruit)
lactuca (a vegetable)
arca (Noah used this.)
monasterium (a religious word)
crispus (Lactuca should be.)
circulus (round and round)
templum (another religious word)
balsamum (a tree)
cometa (Look up for this.)

One scholar has listed a total of 111 English borrowings from Latin in the period from 450 to 650, and

242 more from 650 to 1066, though many of these were not widely used.

A further contribution of the churchmen was writing. Some of them, notably the English Benedictine monk Bede (673–735), wrote extensively, and they also taught some of the English to write, using the Roman alphabet that in modified form we still use. Before this time the Angles, Saxons, and Jutes were mostly illiterate, though some of the "educated" ones had used a runic alphabet. The runes, the letters of this old Germanic alphabet, had generally straight lines that made them easy to carve in wood or stone. For example:

ᚠ (F)	ᛗ (E)	ᚷ (G)
ᛏ (T)	ᛁ (I)	ᛦ (N)
ᚾ (A)	ᚱ (R)	ᛚ (L)

In later years the Roman alphabet, not the runic, was used by Old English writers in composing many of the poems that have survived, including *Beowulf*, one of the world's great epics. Some of England's kings, especially Alfred the Great, who ruled from 871 to 899, encouraged the writing of history, philosophy, and poetry. In the next chapter we'll look at the language used in these writings.

Late in the eighth century still other groups of soldiers began invading the British Isles. The English called them "Danes," although some of them came from other parts of northern Europe and not just from Denmark. At first the Danes merely conducted hit-and-run raids against coastal villages, but then they foraged and plundered farther inland, and eventually some of them settled in England. They did not drive out the English, however, and often lived rather peacefully beside them. The language they spoke was not exactly the same as Old English but was similar enough that the neighbors could understand one another, just as modern Danes, Norwegians, and Swedes may with some effort comprehend one another's language.

Over fourteen hundred place-names in England are of Danish origin, including, for instance, those ending in -*by* (town), -*thwaite* (isolated place), and -*thorp* (village). Examples are *Derby, Rugby, Ormesby, Applethwaite, Braithwaite* (*brai* or *brei* meant "broad"), *Littlethorpe*, and *Thorpe by Water*.

We owe the pronouns *they, their,* and *them* to the Danes; in Old English these all started with *h* (*hīe, hiera, him*). Other borrowings from Danish include a number of words with an *sk* sound: *bask, scare, scrub, skirt, skull, sky, whisk*, etc. Old English used a sound about like that of *y* in many words, but under Danish influence this often changed to a *g* sound, as in *egg, get, give;* if this change had not occurred, modern *yet* and *get* might be pronounced alike, and *give* might be *yive*. Still other borrowings include *bank, call, die, knife, law, low, odd, sister, ugly, window,* and *wrong*.

The Danes became strong enough that in 1014 the king of Denmark, Svein or Sueno, made himself king of England. After his death in the same year he was succeeded, after more fighting, by his son Canute (or Cnut). Canute not only ruled England but also became king of Denmark and Norway. (A famous story about him says that his followers began to regard him as a god. To show them that he was not, he ordered the ocean waves to be still. Since the waves did not obey, he clearly made his point!) Canute remained king until his death in 1035. His two sons, first Harold and then Hardicanute, who succeeded him, had little of their father's genius, and were the last Danish kings of England. In 1042, an Englishman again became king.

The period from 449 to 1066 was the one that established English as the language of the British Isles. Despite the influence of the Roman priests, the Danes, and other people who would come later, the Germanic language of the Angles, Saxons, and Jutes became the base on which Middle and Modern English were to build in centuries to come. In grammar and in basic vocabulary, even though great changes have been made, English is still the language of the Germanic tribes who conquered Britain in the period we have been considering.

▶ Why is Old English sometimes called Anglo-Saxon?

▶ Discuss the appropriateness of the names *England* and *English*. How suitable would it have been to use instead *Celtland* and *Celtish*, for example, or *Romanland* and *Romish* or *Saxonland* and *Saxon*?

▶ Important historical developments are often the result of events outside the territory being considered.

To what extent is this statement true of English history from 449 to 1066?

► Use a good dictionary to identify the languages (Latin or Scandinavian) from which the following words came. Note whether any of the Latin words came from Greek. All of these words were in the English language before the twelfth century.

abbot	leg
alms	martyr
cheese	Mass
chest	meek
creed	mint
dish	(money)
fellow	pound
flat	(weight)
(level)	skin
hit	steak
husband	trivet
keel	trust
kid	want
(young goat)	weak
kitchen	wine

► Choose one of the following subjects and prepare a short report to present to the class.

    a. The runic alphabet (By whom was it used and when? What forms did the letters take? What runic inscriptions still survive?)

b. The Roman alphabet (What was its early history? In what ways does our modern alphabet differ from that of the time of Julius Caesar?)
c. Pictographs, such as those used by American Indians
d. Cuneiform (wedge-shaped) writing
e. Egyptian hieroglyphics
f. The Hebrew right-to-left writing
g. The Cyrillic alphabet of the Russians
h. The Cherokee syllabary of Sequoya
i. The three ways of writing Japanese

3. The Norman Conquest

While England was for centuries being overrun by successive waves of invaders from northern Europe, somewhat the same thing was happening in France. The Northmen (later shortened to *Normans*) came down from Scandinavia and northern Germany and conquered a substantial part of France, an area across the Channel from England. This area, which had its own king, was called Normandy. The Normans intermarried with the French, and a language developed that is known as Norman-French, which replaced the Germanic language originally spoken by the Northmen.

In England, after the Danish Canute's two sons failed as rulers, the English Edward the Confessor became king in 1042. Edward had grown up in Normandy, and he introduced many Norman customs into England. Many Anglo-Saxons did not like this Norman emphasis, and when Edward died in 1066, they managed to put Harold, strongly anti-Norman, on the throne.

The duke of Normandy, named William, a cousin of Edward, thought that he should have been made king of England. Probably King Edward had made him such a promise, and, in addition, at a time when Harold had been a captive in Normandy, he had sworn allegiance to Duke William. With the blessing of the Pope and other European leaders, William took an army across the Channel and, on October 14, 1066, at the famous Battle of Hastings, defeated Harold's army. Harold was killed. After a little over two months of pillaging in southeastern England, William, now called "the Conqueror," was crowned king. The year 1066 is therefore an important one in English history.

William took away the lands of the Anglo-Saxon nobles who had opposed him, and turned them over to his Norman followers. For many years almost all the important positions were held by Normans, and the Anglo-Saxons were often little more than servants or "serfs." Norman merchants took over most of the businesses in London and other large towns.

The English and Norman-French languages existed side by side. English was the language of the "common people," and Norman-French the language of the court, the nobles, most church leaders, and most merchants.

Sir Walter Scott, who wrote in *Ivanhoe* about the period following the Norman Conquest, points out that in general Norman-French words were used to refer to things of higher status than English words were. For example, he has Wamba, the jester in *Ivanhoe*, complain that in talking about dirty animals on the hoof, the Saxons used English names—*cow, calf, ox, sheep, swine,* and *deer;* but when the meats were deliciously prepared, they bore the Norman names *beef, veal, mutton, pork,* and *venison.* Scott also shows Cedric the Saxon asking guests "that you will excuse my speaking to you in my native language, and that you will reply in the same if your knowledge of it permits; if not, I sufficiently understand Norman to follow your meaning." Scott refers too to "the mixed language in which the Norman and Saxon races conversed with each other."

These references of Scott's show three things about the language of this time. The first is that Norman-French words were being added to the vocabulary. Besides the names of meat, there were many others: court words such as *royal, prince, duke, marquis;* legal words such as *attorney, court, crime;* religious words such as *clergy, priest, penitence;* and military words such as *army, corporal, soldier.*

Second, Cedric's statement shows that at least some of the higher-ranking Anglo-Saxons knew both English and Norman-French. When Cedric's Norman visitor responds, "I speak ever French . . . but I understand English sufficiently to communicate with the natives of the country," he is showing that the learning went on in both directions.

Third, the reference to the "mixed language" shows that what had happened repeatedly in Britain was occurring again: the native language and that of the invaders were merging. The changes were not merely in vocabulary but also in grammar and pronunciation. We'll look at these changes in some detail in other chapters.

For about a century and a half French was the language chiefly used by the nobility. But in 1204 the English king lost Normandy, so that the nobles no longer felt strong ties with the Continent. They began to feel "English" instead and to use the English language, though with a large mixture of Norman-French words. By the latter part of the fourteenth century English was the chief language of the schools, although Latin and some French were still used. A law of 1362 required the use of English in lawsuits. Chaucer, the greatest writer of the fourteenth century, chose to write in English. However, a contemporary of his named John Gower was uncertain about which language would finally win out, so he wrote some of his works in English, some in Latin, and some in French.

English survived as well as it did, even in greatly changed form, because the Anglo-Saxons greatly outnumbered the Normans. The Normans had the power, but the Anglo-Saxons had more people. The language that finally resulted from the merger of the two peoples was perhaps 70 or 75 percent derived from Old English and only 25 or so percent from Norman French.

If the Norman Conquest had not occurred, however, the English we speak today might have been quite different in its words, in their pronunciation, in their endings, and possibly in the way they are put together in sentences.

Professor L. M. Myers comments on this point:

> Moreover, the French borrowings were so extensive that they changed the whole balance of the language and prepared the way for the incomparable hospitality to words from other languages that English has shown ever since. The English vocabulary is now much the largest in the world, and well over half of it comes from

French and Latin sources. It is often impossible to tell from which source an originally Latin word was actually borrowed; but even the direct Latin borrowings were certainly made easier by the fact that many French words were already in the language.[1]

► The system of government the Normans had in England is called "feudalism." Read about feudalism in a history or an encyclopedia, and be prepared to discuss how it worked. Also consider the question of how feudal government may have made some contribution to the lingering of the English language and the gradual mixing with Norman-French.

► The following words from the opening lines of Chaucer's *Canterbury Tales* were borrowed by English from French (often Norman-French, but sometimes that of Paris or elsewhere). The words have changed, at least in spelling, since the fourteenth century, but they are still used. Try to guess the modern form of each word.

perced	cours	corage
veyne	melodye	hostelrye
licour	straunge	compaignye
vertu	seson	aventure
tendre	pilgrymage	pilgrimes

---

[1]L. M. Myers, *The Roots of Modern English,* Boston: Little, Brown and Company, 1966, p. 131.

► See what a good dictionary says about the derivation of the following words: *desire, dignity, embrace, horrible, male, mirror, second, sentence.*

► If a word with *ch* was borrowed from French during the Middle Ages, it is usually pronounced today with a *ch* sound as in *chase*. If it was borrowed later, it usually has an *sh* sound as in *machine*. Is each of the following words probably a Middle English borrowing or a later one?

chamber	chant	chevron
chamois	charlatan	chic
champion	chaste	chiffon
chance	chauffeur	choice
change	check	debouch

4. The True-Born Englishman Extends His Reach

We have seen how Celts, Romans, Angles, Saxons, Jutes, Danes, and Normans gradually merged to become the person satirized by Defoe as "the true-born Englishman." There have been no more invasions of the British Isles since 1066 (excluding the bombings of the twentieth century). But England has constantly been engaged in commercial, military, religious, social, or other dealings with foreign countries, and these have inevitably changed the language further.

In the mid-fifteenth century a German, Johann Gutenberg, invented printing from movable type. Previously it had been necessary to copy manuscripts laboriously by hand, one letter at a time. Not only was the process inefficient, but also no two copies would be quite alike. Scribes, for example, spelled each word to suit themselves, since no "correct" spellings existed. The invention of printing led quickly to near standardization in spelling and also in punctuation.

From Germany movable type soon found its way to other countries. The English William Caxton learned about it in Cologne, and in 1475, in Belgium, printed his translation of a book about the Trojan Wars, the first printed English book. Before his death in 1491 (a year before Columbus's discovery of America) Caxton had published about one hundred items, including an encyclopedia called *The Myrrour of the World,* the first illustrated book from an English press. Among his publications was nearly all the English literature that was then in existence, including Chaucer's *Canterbury Tales.* English printing accelerated still more after this fast start, and by 1640 about twenty thousand English books and pamphlets had been printed, plus countless more in Latin and other languages.

The period from about 1400 to 1650 A.D. is known as the Renaissance (also called the Revival of Learning). The invention of printing, more than any other single event, made the Renaissance possible. Scholars and other persons who had a chance to go to school learned a great deal about ancient Greek and Roman literature, art, and culture in general. People who knew Latin and Greek began to use words from those languages, or based on them, in their own writing and speaking. For example, the King James Bible (1611) used *crucified* where earlier English might have used *crossed*, and *prophet* instead of *foresayer*. Some writers borrowed so many long and obscure Latin or Greek words that other writers ridiculed them by imitation, as in this parody by a writer named Thomas Wilson (1553): "Pondering, expending, and revoluting with my selfe, your ingent affabilitie, and ingenious capacity for mundaine affaires: I cannot but celebrate, & extol your magnifical dexteritie above all other." [*Expending* here means "weighing mentally"; *ingent* means "huge."]

Many scholars believed that Greek and Latin were the only great languages, possessing beauty and precision impossible to find in a "vulgar" tongue like English.[2] Some of them tried to improve English by making it look more like Latin. Their zealousness explains how there came to be a *b* in the words *debt* and *doubt,* a *b* that existed in the older Latin words but not in the French *dette* and *doute* that the English had borrowed. For years *fault* had been spelled *faut* or *faute*—without an *l*—but these scholars traced the word back to Latin *fallere* and declared that the English word should preserve the Latin *l*. And *island* (formerly *iland*) has its *s* because of an error: Renaissance scholars incorrectly associated *island* with French *isle,* a word that owed its *s* to the Latin *insula.*

In Shakespeare's time many more Englishmen than before began to travel abroad, particularly on the

---

[2]The term *vulgar,* as used here, does not mean "coarse; indecent." *Vulgar tongue,* an expression widely used for several centuries, simply means "the language of common, ordinary people."

Continent. They brought words back with them, especially from France, Italy, and Spain. Italian, then and later, supplied scores of musical terms, such as *piano, allegro, pizzicato,* and *soprano.* Spanish contributed *desperado, Negro, renegade, mosquito, vanilla,* and many more. The French contributions were the most numerous of all and include many hundreds of words.

English explorers and colonists began to learn about the New World. There they found animals and plants they had not known before. For some of these they adapted native (Indian) names like *raccoon* and *skunk;* for others they coined their own names, like *jack-in-the-pulpit* and *jimson weed.*

As more centuries passed, the British Empire spread around the globe. The boast was that "the sun never sets on the British Empire." The encounters of the English with people in almost every land were both direct and indirect—the indirect encounters being largely by way of foreign literature or international trade. Here are just a few examples of borrowings, some of them at second or third hand, from a variety of tongues:

DUTCH: drawl, gin, deck, cookie

ARABIC: algebra, sugar, zero, giraffe, syrup, harem

PORTUGUESE: anchovy, cobra, molasses, commando, zebra

HEBREW: camel, sapphire, amen, rabbi, cherub

LANGUAGES OF INDIA: bungalow, calico, curry, thug, dungaree

PERSIAN: tulip, khaki, caravan, shawl, bazaar

TURKISH: horde, kiosk, kismet

RUSSIAN: tzar, vodka, mammoth, samovar, pogrom

LANGUAGES OF AFRICA: voodoo, yam, gnu, goober

AMERICAN INDIAN LANGUAGES: chipmunk, pecan, squash, moccasin

CHINESE: chop suey, tong, tea, kumquat, pekoe

JAPANESE: kimono, karate, jujitsu, sukiyaki

The borrowings still go on. A million or so people whom the British call "coloured" have moved into England in recent years; their impact on the language will no doubt gradually become apparent. Then too, if a physicist makes a discovery or an engineer an invention, he is likely to choose a name from what has jokingly been called "Schenectady Greek": *aerostat* and *thermoscope,* for example. If a biologist discovers a previously unknown plant or microbe, he is certain to give it a scientific name taken from Latin or Greek. Thus the first person to give a scientific name to an American elm called it *Ulmus americana* (Latin) and no doubt could have added that it belongs to the phylum *Spermatophyta* (Greek), subphylum *Angiospermae* (Greek), order *Urticales* (Latin), and family *Ulmaceae* (Latin).

Among many new words recorded in the 1973 *Britannica Book of the Year* are such borrowings or adaptations as these:

> *ephebiatrist* (from a Greek word for a person between eighteen and twenty years of age). An ephebiatrist is a doctor who specializes in the medical and psychological treatment of young people.

technethics (Greek *tekhnē* means "art; skill," and Greek *ēthos* means "moral custom"; these roots appear in English words like *technical* and *ethics*.) *Technethics*, says the *Britannica*, is "the responsible use of science, technology, and ethics in a society shaped by technology."

The true-born Englishman, as Defoe said, is "in fact a fiction." In his heredity he is a mixture of many nations and tribes, and perhaps of two or three continents. In his language he is even more mixed, for he has reached to almost all the land areas of earth for contributions. About a fifth of his words are based on Anglo-Saxon; about three fifths are borrowed from Latin or Greek or languages, such as French, that come from Latin; and the remaining fifth come from all parts of the globe.

► On page 51 you learned why there is a *b* in *doubt* and *debt*, an *l* in *fault*, and an *s* in *island*. The *p* in *receipt*, the *b* in *subtle*, and the *c* in *indict* and *verdict* have similar histories. Look up the derivations of these four words and try to figure out how Renaissance scholars justified the inclusion of these letters.

► Try to account for the large number of musical terms borrowed by English from Italian. Try also to account for the borrowing of sailing terms like *sloop* from the Dutch in the sixteenth or seventeenth centuries. Why are borrowings from African languages often the names of animals—*chimpanzee* and *okapi*, for instance?

► Sometimes when a word is borrowed, it changes in meaning. For example, *confetti* to most of us means "small bits of colored paper to throw at weddings or parades," but to most Italians it means "sugar-covered almonds." Look up the following words in your dictionary to find out what each meant in the language or languages from which it was derived.

carouse	cruise
rodeo	assassin
piano	muscle
mosquito	abundance

► If the class has a large map of the world or a large globe to which slips of paper may be pasted, it may be interesting to show the lands from which various English words have come. The list on pages 52–53 will give you a beginning, which can be supplemented by the following list plus other words the members of the class look up. Paste in appropriate spots on the map or globe slips of paper with the words written or typed on them.

You will often find two or more languages listed as sources of a word; for example, *pumpkin* is from Middle French, Latin, and Greek. When this occurs, place the labels in each source country—France, Italy, and Greece for *pumpkin*. You may need to search a little further and then use your best judgment when you encounter sources like Algonquian and Nahuatl.

alcohol	kangaroo	seraph
barbecue	kudu	sombrero
blitz	lei	tomahawk
bolshevik	lemon	trek
boomerang	llama	tub
chocolate	polka	turquoise
coyote	polo	tycoon
ghetto	pumpkin	violin
gingham	robot	wigwam
jazz	samurai	yen

► For discussion: In what ways might the inventing of printing affect a language?

3

the
language
of
king
alfred
the
great

In Chapter 1 we looked at relatives and ancestors of the English language. In Chapter 2 we traced the ways in which English, through the centuries, built upon and was influenced by other languages. Now we are ready to go back and get a closer view of what the English language looked like a thousand years ago, when only a part of the mixing had taken place.

1. Some Examples of Old English

If you look carefully at a picture taken in early childhood of yourself or one of your friends or an older person, you often can see many points of resemblance as well as of difference between the picture and the present appearance. The chin line or the brow line may be about the same, or the proportionate size of the ears, or the color of the eyes, or the shape of the smile. But there may be differences in hair color, proportionate eye size, bodily shape, or other features.

It's much the same with language. A comparison of an early and a late variety will reveal many similarities and many differences.

The purpose of this section is not to teach you to read Old English (although it may suggest that with some effort you *could* read it). Rather, the purpose is to provide some examples of Old English *(OE)* and to glance at how they are both like and different from Modern English *(Mod E)*.

Let's start with some short bits that resemble Modern English fairly closely. The first is one of a large number of laws proclaimed by the sixth-century King Ethelbert of Kent; it tells the size of the fine for a particular offense:

> Gif man ōþerne mid fȳste in naso slæhð, III scillinga.

Before reading further, see how much of that law you can interpret for yourself.

You probably got *man, fist, in,* and *three shillings* (the amount of the fine), and perhaps guessed that the law had something to do with hitting someone with a fist. If you were alert enough to remember *nasal* and think about the probable landing place of the fist, you may have translated *naso* as *nose*. Now you have:

> Gif man ōþerne mid fist in nose slæhð, three shillings.

Gif rather clearly has today been reduced to *if*. Perhaps you recall from an earlier chapter that both þ and ð are OE symbols for *th; ōþerne* thus becomes *otherne*, which suggests *other*. You settle tentatively on that and move on to *mid*. The context of *fist* in *nose* suggests that *mid* probably means "with," and if you happen to know that in German *with* is *mit*, that suspicion is confirmed.

All you have left is *slæhð*, which doesn't look much easier as *slæhth*. Again context helps. The law must say something about hitting somebody in the nose, so *slæhð* probably means "hits." (Actually, this verb is the ancestor of our *slay*, and in Old English it could mean either "strike" or "slay.")

We put the pieces together and find that we have:

> If man other with fist in nose hits, three shillings.

That's a bit rough, so we add a little Mod E polish:

> If a man hits another in the nose with his fist, three shillings.

The heading for all these fines prescribed by King Ethelbert reads as follows:

> Þis syndon þa dōmas þe Æðelbirht cyning āsette on Augustīnus dæge.

These clues should help you read that sentence:

þis = these
þa = the
dōmas = penalties ("dooms")
þe = that

61

cyning: What was Æðelbirht's title?
āsette = ásettę

Don't be surprised, though, later on when you find
that the word for *that* may be *þæt* or something else,
or that *the* may be *þon* or another word. Such differences may be partly dialectal, but mainly they are due
to the fact that adjectives and words like *the* changed
form to harmonize with their nouns.

Here is King Alfred's version of two of the biblical
Ten Commandments. They are easy to translate,
given the clue that *ū* often became *ou* in later English,
and that *sleah* is another form of *slæhð* (p. 61).

Nē sleah ðū.
Nē stala ðū.

Caedmon was the earliest known English Christian poet. He was a poor herdsman who once left a
party early because the guests had been told that each
would have to entertain by singing—that is, composing
and singing verses. Later that night in a dream a
stranger appeared before him and said,

"Cedmon, sing mē hwætwugu (something)."
Þā (Then) ondswarede hē ond cwæð (quoth *or* said):
"Ne con ic (I) nōht (not at all) singan."

The stranger persuaded him to try, and

Þā cwæð hē, "Hwæt sceal ic singan?"
Cwæð hē, "Sing mē frumsceaft (creation)."

So Caedmon composed a famous hymn about the
creation of the world, and later on great numbers of

other religious poems, which unfortunately have vanished.

Now let's turn to a longer passage. King Alfred—a remarkable man with wide interests—wrote it about a voyage made in the ninth century by a Norwegian Viking, Ohthere (pronounced about like "oak-there"). Ohthere's path would be easy to trace on a map of northern Europe. He started from northwest Norway, proceeded north and then east along the coast in the frigid waters of the Arctic Ocean, moved past the wide and bleak expanse of Lapland, headed south into the White Sea of Russia, and (probably) went into the funnel-shaped channel that modern maps label Kandalakshskiy Zal. It was one of the many daring voyages by the Vikings that prepared the way for their discovery of the New World a couple of centuries later.

► Try your hand at "translating" the passage to present-day English. The words you are unlikely to know or be able to guess have been defined. However, you will sometimes still need to change the word order or add a word like *the* or *a* or make some other adjustments, in order to have a fairly smooth translation. When you have finished, compare your translation with the one on pages 205–206. (At this time, ignore the marks above certain vowels. You will use them later in practicing pronunciation.)

                 [to]   *lord*
Ōhthere sǣde   his hlāforde, Ælfrēde cyninge,

of all   *northmost lived*
þæt hē ealra Norðmonna norþmest būde. Hē cwæð

     the
þæt hē būde on þæm lande norþweardum

by the West Sea   *though*
wiþ þā Westsæ. Hē sæde þēah þæt þæt land

is [or *stretches*] *very far*   *thence yet*
sīe   swīþe lang norþ þonan; ac hit is

all waste except that *in few*   *places*
eal wēste,   būton   on fēawum stōwum

here and there camp Finns for hunting
styccemælum wīciað Finnas, on huntoðe on wintra,

      fishing in the
ond on sumera on fiscaþe be þære sæ.

      one   *time wanted to find*
Hē sæde þæt hē æt sumum cirre wolde fandian

how far   *straight north lay*   *or*
hū longe þæt land norþryhte   læge, oþþe hwæðer

any   *to*   *of the wasteland*   *Then went*
ænig mon be norðan þæm wēstenne būde. Þā fōr

    along the   *Kept he all the way*
hē norþryhte be þæm lande. Lēt him ealne weg

waste   *starboard*   *open sea*
þæt wēste land on ðæt stēorbord, ond þā wīdsæ

  larboard   *days Then*   *as far*
on ðæt bæcbord þrīe dagas. Þā wæs hē swā feor

  the whalehunters farthest go   *went*
norþ swā þā hwælhuntan firrest faraþ. Þā fōr hē

still   *might*
þā gīet norþryhte swā feor swā hē meahte on þǣm

next three   *days*   *sail*   *turned*
ōþrum þrīm dagum gesiglan. Þā bēag þæt land

there straight east   *or*   *the*
þǣr ēastryhte,   oþþe sēo sǣ in on ðæt lond,

knew not   *which* *but*   *knew*
hē   nysse   hwæðer; būton hē wisse ðæt hē ðǣr

waited for   *somewhat northerly*
bād   westanwindes ond hwōn norþan,

sailed   *along*   *as far as*
ond siglde ðā ēast be lande swā swā hē meahte on

four   *must*   *wait for*
fēower dagum gesiglan. Þā sceolde hē ðǣr bīdan

straight north wind because   *turned*
ryhtnorþanwindes, for ðǣm þæt land bēag þǣr

straight south
sūþryhte,   oþþe sēo sǣ in on ðæt land, hē nysse

            thence   *near*
hwæþer. Þā siglde hē þonan sūðryhte be lande swā

    might   *lay*
swā hē mehte on fīf dagum gesiglan. ðā læg þǣr

a great river   *turned they*
ān micel ēa ūp in on þæt land. Þā cirdon hīe ūp in

      because   *not dared past by the*
on ðā ēa, for þǣm hīe ne dorston forþ bī þǣre ēa

sail   *because of hostility*
siglan   for   unfriþe, for þǣm ðæt land wæs

inhabited   side   of the river Nor had met
eall gebūn on ōþre healfe þǣre ēas. Ne mētte

previously any   since
   hē ǣr   nān gebūn   land, siþþan hē from his

own   home went But for him   all the
āgnum hām fōr.   Ac him   wæs ealne weg

                              except for fishermen
wēste land on þæt stēorbord,   būtan   fiscerum

   fowlers   they
ond fugelerum ond huntum, ond þæt wǣron eall

        for him   an
Finnas; ond him wæs ā wīdsǣ on ðæt bæcbord.

▶ In reading the King Alfred passage, one thing you
probably noticed was that the same word was not
always spelled in the same way. *The*, for instance, was
þǣm, þā, þǣre, þǣt, and *sēo*. Find some other
examples.

Sometimes the differences in OE spelling are due
simply to the fact that spelling had not yet been standardized, since printing had not yet been invented.
More often, however, the differences stem from the
fact that many OE words had several forms, and one
form was to be used in one set of circumstances, other
forms in others. Thus *dagas* (days) was the regular
form for the subject or object, but after a preposition
the form was often *dagum*.

Another point you may have noticed is that King Alfred's word order is often not the same as ours. We would say "Finns camp in a few places," but he said "in a few places camp Finns"; we would say "whether any man lives to the north of the wasteland," but Alfred said "whether any man to the north of the wasteland lives."

► Find other examples of the unusual word order used in the King Alfred passage.

The main reason for the difference in word order was that OE words had inflectional endings that made the meaning easy to recognize even if the arrangement was a little unusual. Later most of the inflectional endings would be lost, and the word order would become relatively fixed. The two changes occurred together, and each aided the other. When the order became fixed, inflections were not needed to show, for instance, whether a noun was a subject or an object. If a person said, "The dog bit the mailman," the order revealed the intended meaning; special endings were no longer necessary to show who did the biting and who got bit. Natually, then, the OE endings on such words tended to be dropped.

As a final example of Old English, let's look at a few lines from the earliest English epic, *Beowulf*. The manuscript dates from about 1000 A.D., but the poem probably was actually composed (by an unknown author) in the early eighth century. The first major episode of the poem concerns a fight between the hero, Beowulf, and a monster called Grendel that nightly has been killing the warriors of King Hrōðgār.

In the selection, Beowulf has just come from across the sea and is introducing himself to Hrōðgār and his followers. The translation given here is a rather free one, not word for word.

Beowulf spoke   *—on him the coat of mail shone,*
Bēowulf maðelode   —on him byrne scān,

chain armor linked   *by the skill of the smith:*
searonet seowed   smiþes orþancum:

"Good health to you, Hrothgar!
"Wæs þū, Hrōðgār, hāl!
                    I am [King] Higelac's
                    Ic eom Higelāces

kinsman and young follower.
mǣg ond magoðegn.
                    I have many glorious deeds
                    Hæbbe ic mǣrða fela

undertaken in my youth.
ongunnen on geogoþe.
                    To me became the affair of Grendel
                    Mē wearð Grendles þing

in my native soil   *clearly known.*
on mīnre ēþeltyrf   undyrne cūð.

You will notice that rhyme is not normally involved in OE poetry, although sometimes a poet would use a little of it for special effect. Each line, however, usually has five accented syllables, in that way being like the pentameter line that has since been a favorite of English poets; a five-beat line is used, for instance, in Shakespeare's plays and in Milton's blank-verse *Paradise Lost*. Each line in *Beowulf* can be divided into two half-lines, as is done above; either two or three of the accented syllables may be in each half-line.

Every line has alliteration—the repetition of the same sound in accented syllables in the two half-lines. Note in the first line Beowulf—byrne; in the second, searonet seowed—smiþes. The pattern could be one and one, as in the first line; two and one, as in the second; one and two; two and two; or, though rarely, three and one, one and three, three and two, two and three, or even three and three.

► What are the alliterative sounds and their patterns in the last four lines of the *Beowulf* passage? (The final line uses *vowel* alliteration: any vowel sound could be alliterated with any other; it didn't have to be the *same* vowel.)

2. Pronunciation of Old English

Since more than a thousand years were to elapse before Thomas Edison invented the phonograph, we have no recordings to show us exactly how Old English was pronounced. However, scholars have pieced together hundreds of bits of evidence and can tell us fairly confidently what the words sounded like. We can be much less sure about the speech rhythms.

The sounds described below are those of early Old English. By the time of the Norman Conquest (1066) some changes had appeared. It should also be noted that the sounds differed somewhat in various dialects.

These consonants were pronounced about as they are today:

```
p    t    m    l    x
b    d    n    w
```

So you have nine sounds already that will give you no trouble. And since the OE alphabet did not have *j*, *q*, *v*, or *z*, you don't have to worry about those.

F was usually like our *f*. The word *flōr* (floor), for instance, was pronounced like its modern equivalent. But between vowels, *f* had a *v* sound; thus *drīfan* (drive) was pronounced "dree-vahn."

S was usually like Mod E *s* in *so*. *Sittan* (sit) was "sit-tahn." Between vowels, though, the *s* was like Mod E *z*, so that *rīsan* (rise) was "ree-zahn."

The Anglo-Saxons apparently curved back the tip of the tongue in pronouncing *r* so that a somewhat trilled sound resulted. This may be difficult for an untrained tongue; you may want to practice on *rīsan* and *rād* (raid). Try saying "rree-zahn" and "rrahd."

C was generally like Mod E *k*. Practice on *clif* (cliff) and *brocen* (broken). *Clif* was about the same as Mod E *cliff*, but the *e* in *brocen* was pronounced a little more distinctly than we do it: "bro-kehn." But sometimes *c* was like Mod E *ch* as in *church*. Practice on *cēowan* (chew) and *cīdan* (chide). Say "chay-oh-wahn" and "chee-dahn."

Sc was about like Mod E *sh*. Try *sceal* (shall) and *fisc* (fish). Say "sheh-ahl" and "fish."

Cg was like the *j* of Modern English. Now that you can pronounce OE *ecg*, you know what its present-day form must be.

G is a tricky one. It could be either like Mod E *g* in *go* or *y* in *yet* or like the *g* in Modern North German *sagen* (that's what makes it tricky). Without much trouble you can pronounce *nigon* (nine) and *hungor* (hunger) by saying "nig-on" and "hoong-gawr" (*oo* as in *foot*). Also *gīt* (yet) and *geolu* (yellow) are not hard to say as "yeet" and "yay-oh-luh." But the third *g* sound, unless you're a North German or a reincarnated Anglo-Saxon, may be impossible for you. Two experts say the way to do it is "by relaxing the contact between the tongue and the roof of the mouth while one pronounces the *g* of Modern *goose*." Then they add this comforting footnote: "If one is unable to acquire this sound he may substitute for it the stop *g* in Modern English *goose*."[1] Try it on *boga* (bow) "boe-gah" and on *gēs* (geese) "gace."

H was often like Mod E *h*. *Hē* (he) was "hay," and for *hring* (ring), just say "hring." In Mod E *what* and *while*, despite the spelling, we pronounce first the *h* and then the *w*. So did Angles and Saxons in *hwæt* and *hwīl*, only their spelling was here more logical than ours. Say "hwat" (with *a* as in *cat*) and "hweel." Sometimes, though, the *h* was like German *ch* in *ich*—a kind of *k* sound with a longer expulsion of breath. This may be difficult for you unless you know German, but you may practice on *niht* (night) "nikt" and *sōhte* (sought) "soak-tuh."

---

[1]Samuel Moore and Thomas A. Knott. *The Elements of Old English*, Ann Arbor: George Wahr, 1942. p. 14.

OE vowels	Pronunciations
a	as in Mod E *art*
ā	as in Mod E *calm* (held longer time than **a**)
æ	as in Mod E *at*
ǣ	as in Mod E *care*
e	as in Mod E *bend*
ē	nearly like *a* in Mod E *late*
i	as in Mod E *it*
ī	as in Mod E *machine*
o	as in Mod E *omit*
ō	nearly like *o* in Mod E *alone* (held longer time than **o**)
u	nearly like *oo* in Mod E *foot*
ū	nearly like *u* in Mod E *rule*
y	about like German *ü* in *dünn* or French *u* in *tu*
ȳ	like German *ü* in *kühn* or French *u* in *lune*
ea	æ + a, later æ + ə (a brief "uh" sound)
ēa	ǣ + a, later ǣ + ə
eo	e + o, later e + ə
ēo	ē + o, later ē + ə
ie	i + e, later i + ə
īe	ī + e, later ī + ə

Ng was pronounced like Mod E *ng* in *finger,* not as in *ringer.* Practice on *singan* (sing) "sing-gahn" and *ðing* (thing) "thing-g."

The OE letter *þ,* called thorn, and the letter *ð,* called eth, could both be pronounced like either the *th* of Mod E *thin* or the *th* of *then.* The first of these sounds is called "unvoiced" or "voiceless" because the vocal cords don't vibrate; the second is called "voiced" because they do. You can test the difference by placing your thumb and forefinger lightly on

72

OE examples (with meanings)

ac (but); faran (to travel)
āc (oak); stān (stone)
æt (at); dæg (day)
ænig (any); hwǣr (where)
ende (end); fela (many)
hē (he); grētan (to greet)
in (in); swilc (such)
tīd (time); rīdan (to ride)
ofer (over); gold (gold)
gōd (good); ōðer (other)

under (under); full (full)
hūs (house); lūcan (to close)
ymbe (about); cynn (kin)

cȳðan (to make known)
eall (all); earm (arm)
hēah (high); bēam (tree)
eorðe (earth); seolh (seal)
ēower (your); frēond (friend)
hierde (herder)
hīeran (to hear)

---

your neck muscles as you pronounce first the *th* of *thin* and second the *th* of *then;* you should feel vibration only the second time.

The þ or ð sound was unvoiced at the beginning or the end of a word and between certain consonants, but voiced between vowels and between certain other consonants. The double þþ or ðð was unvoiced. For the voiceless sound, pronounce *ðing* again, as well as *mūþ* (mouth) "mooth" and *moþþe* (moth) "mo-thuh." For the voiced sound, try *cweðan* (say) "kwehthahn" and *eorðe* (earth) "eh-or-thuh." English still does peculiar things with the *th* sound; we have, for example, such pairs as *south* (unvoiced) but *southern* (voiced), *worth* (unvoiced) but *worthy* (voiced).

Some of the vowel pronunciations have been indicated in the examples you have been trying. The table[2] at the top of pages 72 and 73, which provides vowel markings, shows all of the sounds of the various vowels.

► Try pronouncing all the words given as examples. The purpose is not to make you perfect in OE pronunciation, but merely to give you some idea about how our pronunciations have changed in the last thousand years. You may want to work with a partner or in a small group, checking each other's pronunciation against the descriptions given above. In working on the vowel sounds, remember also to pronounce the consonants in the ways described.

You will notice that some pronunciations have hardly changed at all. The vowel sounds in *gold*, *æt*, *in*, and *full*, for example, are in Modern English almost the same as in Old English. In other vowel sounds a regular shift occurred that we'll look at more carefully later. An example is in the *ū* words, where *hūs* became *house*, *mūs* became *mouse*, *ðū* became *thou*, *mūþ* became *mouth*, and *hū* became *how*.

---

[2]George T. Flom, *Old English Grammar and Reader*, Boston: D. C. Heath & Co., 1930, p. 10. Reprinted by permission of the Publisher.

▶ You may also want to try pronouncing the words in a few lines of the Ohthere story or the excerpt from *Beowulf*. The so-called long vowels have been marked to help you. One thing to remember is that final *e*'s were not silent in Old English; thus *wēste* is "way-stuh," not just Mod E "waste."

3. Old English Grammar

This section will answer such questions as these:

Why do we say *feet* rather than *foots*, and *deer* rather than *deers*?
Did the language ever have a word meaning "the two of us"?
Why do some people say *hit* for *it*?
Why do we say "My feet are frozen" instead of "My feet are freezed"?
How does it happen that *-ly* is the usual ending for adverbs?

Nouns. You will recall that English, like other Indo-European languages, has inflections. That is, it has endings like *-s* and *-ed* that show plurality or case or tense or something else. Old English was much more highly inflected than English is today, but less so than Latin, Greek, Sanskrit, or some other Indo-European languages.

As an example of OE inflections, consider *stān* (stone). In Modern English this word has the forms *stone, stone's, stones,* and *stones'*—four written forms and two pronunciations. In Old English there were more:

Nominative and accusative singular	stān
Genitive (possessive) singular	stānes
Dative singular	stāne
Nominative and accusative plural	stānas
Genitive (possessive) plural	stāna
Dative plural	stānum

The nominative and accusative forms were used as subjects and direct objects, the genitives were used mainly to show possession, and the datives (which have disappeared entirely in Modern English) were used for indirect objects and after most prepositions.

The reason for some of our irregular Mod E plurals can be traced to Old English. For example, *oxen* goes back to the OE form *oxan*. The explanation of the *r* in *children* lies in the OE plural *cildru*. The OE plurals of *fōt* (foot), *gōs* (goose), *tōþ* (tooth), and *mann* (man) were *fēt*, *gēs*, *tēþ*, and *menn*. Interestingly enough, the plural of Mod E *book* could very easily have been *beek*, since the OE plural was *bēc*.

The reason why *deer*, *sheep*, and some other words do not have *s* plurals is that in Old English the singular and plural forms were alike. Thus *dēor* (deer), which in Old English meant almost any kind of wild animal, was also *dēor* in the plural. If it had not been for a later change, the following words would also have had the same singular and plural forms in Modern English, since they did in Old English: *word, year, chin, house, land, sword,* and *thing*.

There is some evidence that inflectional endings were being lost or merged with one another before the coming of the Normans. One reason may be that the Danes and the Anglo-Saxons did not use exactly the same inflections, so in speaking with one another, they perhaps tended to blur and eventually to blend the endings. Then, when the Normans ruled England, they did not want to bother to learn the inflections, and as a result many of the endings became a vague "uh" sound or disappeared entirely. Similarly, when American soldiers were stationed in Italy after World War II, they usually ignored the Italian endings, and in conversation with Americans, some of the Italians did the same thing. If the Americans had remained and had intermarried, chances are that in a couple of centuries Italian would lose many of its numerous inflectional endings.

Pronouns. One of the features of OE pronouns was the existence of a "dual" number as well as a singular and plural. If Modern English had this same feature, when we wanted to say "us two" or "you two" we'd use a single-word pronoun pronounced something like "unk" or "yit."

Here is what the first-person pronouns were:

	SINGULAR	DUAL	PLURAL
Nominative	ic	wit	wē
Genitive	mīn	uncer	ūre
Dative	mē	unc	ūs
Accusative	mē	unc	ūs

Mīn and *ūre*, the singular and plural genitives, had a number of different forms. *My* developed later, and for a long time afterward *mine* continued to be used before vowel sounds, as in "Mine eyes have seen the glory." The dialectal word *ourn*, as in "These

77

rabbits are *ourn*," is a survival of one form of the accusative—*ūrne*.

Here are the case forms of the OE second-person pronouns:

Nominative	þū	git	gē
Genitive	þīn	incer	ēower
Dative	þē	inc	ēow
Accusative	þē	inc	ēow

► What do you suppose *þū*, *þīn*, and *þē* became in later years? Try to figure out what now old-fashioned word the pronoun *gē* became. What do you suppose is the modern spelling of *ēow?* of *ēower?* (Pronouncing the OE words may help you figure out the answers.)

The third-person pronouns had no dual number:

SINGULAR

	Masculine	Feminine	Neuter
Nominative	hē	hēo	hit
Genitive	his	hire	his
Dative	him	hire	him
Accusative	hine	hīe	hit

PLURAL FOR ALL THREE GENDERS

Nominative	hīe or hī
Genitive	hira or hiera or heora
Dative	him
Accusative	hīe or hī

The way that *hēo* became *she* is not definitely known; but it may have been caused by a combination with *sēo*, a feminine word for *the*. Scandinavian influence accounts for our *th* in *they* and *them*. The pronunciation *hit* for *it* is still heard in some parts of England and in backwoods areas of the United States.

Among the OE pronouns for asking questions was *hwā* (who), with a possessive *hwæs* (whose) and a dative *hwǣm* or *hwām*, the ancestor of *whom*. Our *why* developed from *hwȳ*, one form of *hwā*. *Hwæt* was the OE form of *what*. *Hwæðer* was used to ask "Which of two?" and *hwilc* (the ancestor of *which*) to ask "Which of several?"

Adjectives.   In Modern English an adjective always has the same form, except in comparisons. So we say "*Good* music appeals to me," "The sound of *good* music appeals to me," "I like *good* music," and so on, with *good* never changing in form.

Not so in Old English. *Gōd* (good), like other adjectives, had to agree with its noun. When its noun was masculine and singular and possessive, the form *gōdes* was used, but for feminine singular possessive the form was *gōdre*. When the word for *the* was used with the adjective and noun, a different form of *gōd* was required. Plural forms differed from singular. In all, ten different forms of *gōd* existed, and the correct form had to be found to fit any of about fifty possible situations. So the use of the adjective was infinitely more complex than in Modern English.

You may wonder how speakers of the language mastered such complexity. They had no grammar books, and if there had been any, the written rules would have taken a long time to learn and still longer to apply. But remember that Anglo-Saxon children grew up with the language, hearing it constantly even in the cradle. Through hearing and imitation they learned that one said "gōd mann" in one situation, "gōdes mannes" in another, "gōde menn" in another, and "þāra gōdra manna" in still another. The form and use of the noun determined the form of the adjective.

Primitive languages are often much more complicated than civilized languages. Small children learn these complex languages as quickly as other children learn relatively simple ones.

But older people have more difficulty. So the adult Danes and Normans, when they tried to learn Old English, would often learn *gōd* but not the various endings. Slowly, therefore, the endings were lost.

Verbs. Somewhat the same situation existed in OE verbs. They were either "strong" or "weak," with the weak ones more numerous. The strong verbs, like Mod E *sing, sang, sung,* changed the vowel for the past tense and the past participle. The weak verbs, like Mod E *walk, walked, walked,* formed the past tense by adding *-ede, -ode,* or *-de,* and formed the past participle by adding *-ed, -od,* or *-d.* The strong verbs were subdivided into seven groups, depending on the vowel changes involved.

Most of what are called "irregular" verbs in Modern English are descended from OE strong verbs. This is why we say *wrote* and *written* instead of *writed, sang* and *sung* instead of *singed, stole* and *stolen* instead of *stealed, took* and *taken* instead of *taked, froze* and *frozen* instead of *freezed, blew* and *blown* instead of *blowed,* etc. Our "regular" verbs have past tenses and participles with *-ed* (or sometimes *-t,* as in *dreamt*).

► Which of the following Mod E verbs would you guess were strong in Old English?

ask	spring	live
ride	hold	grow
run	look	begin
talk	drive	paint
declare	give	eat

Here are the present and past tenses of an OE strong verb, *wrītan* (to write):

PRESENT		PAST	
Singular	Plural	Singular	Plural
ic wrīte	wē wrītað	ic wrāt	wē writon
þū wrītst	gē wrītað	þū write	gē writon
hē wrīteð	hīe wrītað	hē wrāt	hīe writon

Other forms were used for the subjunctive mood. The imperative singular was *wrīt*, plural *wrītað*. The form corresponding to our present participle *writing* was *wrītende*, and the past participle, our *written*, could be *writen* or *gewriten*.

In contrast, the weak verb *ferian* (to carry) had *ferede* as the basic past tense form; note the *d* that characterizes the past of weak verbs both in Old English and Modern English. The past of *fyllan* (to fill) was *fylde;* of *rīcsian* (to rule), *rīcsode*.

Some verbs that were strong in Old English have become weak. You may have heard a speaker of a certain dialect say "He *clumb* a tree" or "He *holp* me last night," where you would say *climbed* and *helped*. His choices go back to Old English, when the words for *climb* and *help* were strong verbs and had past tense forms corresponding to *clumb* and *holp*.

Adverbs.   Although OE adverbs were not all formed in the same way, a number of them were created by adding -*līce* (pronounced "lee-chuh") to an adjective. Here's how it worked: A noun like *frēond* (friend) was changed first to an adjective by adding -*līc* (like), so that *frēondlīc* was the adjective (friendlike). Then, to make an adverb, -*e* was added, giving *frēondlīce* (in a friendlike manner). Later, the -*līce* ending was attached even to adjectives that didn't come from nouns. Thus *eornost* (earnest) plus -*līce* gave *eornost-līce* (earnestly).

This -*līce* is the ancestor of the Mod E -*ly* that serves as the ending of most of our adverbs. If someone strikes *savagely*, he strikes "like a savage." If someone feels *deeply*, he feels "deeplike."

▶ What are the basic meanings of *strongly, desperately, shamefully, skillfully, angrily?*

This quick view of OE grammar has omitted prepositions, conjunctions, and interjections, as well as sentence structure. It should, however, have given you some understanding of the great reliance of Old

English on inflectional endings, and it has suggested the reasons for some of the oddities of Mod E grammar.

4

the language of chaucer

THE date customarily given for the beginning of Middle English is 1100 A.D. You must remember, though, that language change is gradual and that such dates can only be approximate. Obviously the English people did not wake up on January 1, 1100, and say, "Today we shall stop speaking Old English and start speaking Middle English." In fact, they did not know that the language they had been speaking was "Old," and Chaucer's fourteenth-century friends did not know that theirs was "Middle." These terms, plus "Modern," are only convenient labels.

► Do you suppose that our descendants in 3000 A.D. will call twentieth-century English "Modern"? What may they call it instead?

Despite the necessary cautiousness about dates, scholars generally designate as "Middle English" *(ME)* the English spoken between 1100 and 1500. This was a period of continued change in the language. In 1100, English was essentially the Old English we looked at in Chapter III, but by 1500 it had changed enough that it rather closely resembled the English of today.

Most of our discussion in this chapter will deal with the Middle English of the fourteenth century— neither very early nor very late. One reason is that one of England's great literary figures, Geoffrey Chaucer (1340?–1400), lived in this century. Another is that the fourteenth century is just beyond the midpoint of Middle English and therefore is especially representative of the four-hundred-year span.

1. Some Examples of Middle English

Let us look first at a few lines from a long thirteenth-century poem, *Brut*, composed in about 1205 by a priest named Layamon. Layamon was the first person to write in English the stories of King Arthur and his knights of the Round Table, devoting about ten thousand lines to this subject. The selection concerns King Arthur's last words as he lay dying on the battlefield. You should be able to read it with the help of the clues provided.

          sorely wounded   *wonderfully much*
Arður wes forwunded   wunder ane swiðe.

            boy   *kin*
þerto him com a cnave   þe wes of his cunne.

           son
He wes Cadores sune,   þe eorles of Cornwale.

         was called
Constantin hehte þe cnave.

                     to the
             He wes þan kinge deore.

                        [the] ground
Arður him lokede on   þer he lai on   folden,

   these   *sorrowful*
And þas word seide   mid sorhfulle heorte:

"Constantin, þu art wilcume;
                     þu weore Cadores sone.

   to you bequeath   *kingdom*
Ich þe   bitache here   mine kineriche,

   guard   *Britons always*
And wite mine Bruttes a   to þine lifes ende,

   uphold for them   *laws*
And hald   heom   alle þa lagen

             have   stood in   days
           þa habbeoð istonden a mine dagen,

And alle þa lagen gode

              [*King*] *Uther's*
        þa bi   Uðeres   dagen stode.

       fare   *Avalon*
And ich wulle varen to Avalun,

            [*the*] *fairest of all*
        to vairest alre   maidene,

            fairy extremely beautiful
To Argante þere quene,   alven swiðe   sceone,

   she   *wounds*   *sound*
And heo scal mine wunden   makien alle isunde

Also whole   *healing draughts*
Al   hal   me makien   mid haleweige drenchen.

    afterward
And   seðe   ich cumen wulle   to mine kineriche

    live   *joy*
And wunien mid Brutten   mid muchelere wunne."

▶ In comparing the Layamon passage with the Old English of Chapter 3, do you find that more or fewer of the words resemble Modern English? Are the sounds of *th* still indicated as in Old English? Is alliteration used in the poetry as in Old English? Find several sentences or parts of sentences in which the word order is the same as in Modern English (for example, "He wes Cadores sune").

The next selection is from *The Travels of Sir John Mandeville*, a strange collection of travel legends written originally in French by a Liège physician, John de Bourgoyne or Jehan de la Barbe (John with the beard). The book was extremely popular and was translated into English in about 1377 or perhaps a little later. A modern reader can read much of it with little help.

There is a vale betwene the mountaynes, that dureth nyghe a [*extends almost*] 4 myle; and summen clepen [*call*] it the vale enchaunted, some clepen it the vale of Develes, and some clepen it the vale perilous. In that vale heren [*hear*] men often tyme grete tempestes and thondres, and grete murmures and noyses, alle dayes and nyghtes; and gret noyse, as it were sown [*sounds*] of tabours [*tabors, small drums*] and of nakeres [*nakers, kettledrums*] and of trompes [*trumpets*], as thoughe it were of a gret feste. This vale is alle fulle of develes, and hathe ben alle weys. And men seyn there that it is on [*one*] of the entrees of helle. . . . And thus wee passeden that perilouse vale, and founden thereinne gold and sylver and precious stones and riche jewelles gret plentee, both here and there, as us semed [*as it seemed to us*]; but whether that it was as us semede, I wot nere [*I do not know*], for I touched none, because that the develes ben so subtyle to make a thing to seme otherwise than it is, for to disceyve mankynde, and therefore I touched none; and also because that I wolde not ben put out of my devocioun, for I was more devout thanne, than evere I was before or after, and alle for the drede of fendes [*fiends*] that I saughe in dyverse figures; and also for the gret multytude of dede bodyes that I saughe there liggynge be [*along*] the weye be [*through*] alle the vale, as thoughe there had ben a bataylle betwene 2 kynges and the myghtyest of the contree, and that the gretter partye had ben discomfyted and slayn.

▶ Perhaps you have seen the old word *yclept*, meaning "called" or "named." What word in the passage above seems to be related?

▶ Note the numerous words ending in *e*. This was not generally a silent *e* in Middle English but was pronounced somewhat like "uh." It represents the OE endings, many of which had been reduced to this vague sound. Try pronouncing the words.

▶ In relation to word order, what similarities and differences do you notice between this passage and Modern English?

▶ What words do you see that are exactly like their Mod E equivalents? Which are apparently the same except for differences in spelling (and of course in pronunciation)?

We'll now look at a few verses from the first complete translation of the Bible, by John Wycliffe, who was born about 1320. For purposes of comparison and clarification, we follow it with the same verses from the King James Bible of 1611.

1. In that day Jhesus going out of the hous, sat besidis the see.
2. And manye cumpanyes of peple ben gadrid to hym, so that he steying vp in a boot sat; and al the cumpanye stode in the brynke.
3. And he spak to hem many thingis in parablis, seiyinge, Loo! he that sowith goth out to sowe his seed.
4. And the while he soweth, sum felden beside the weye, and briddes of the eyre camen, and eeten hem.
5. Sothely other seedis felden into stoony placis, wher thei hadden nat moche erthe; and anoon thei ben sprungen up, for thei hadde nat depnesse of erthe.
6. Sothely the sunne sprung up, thei swaliden, or brenden for hete, and for thei hadden nat roote, thei drieden vp.
7. Forsothe other seedis felden amonge thornis; and the thornis wexen vp, and strangliden hem.
8. But other seedis felden in to good lond, and gaven fruyt; sume an hundred fold, another sexti fold, another thritti fold.
9. He that hath eris of heerynge, heere he.

*   *

1. The same day went Jesus out of the house, and sat by the sea side.

2. And great multitudes were gathered together unto him, so that he went into a ship, and sat; and the whole multitude stood on the shore.
3. And he spake many things unto them in parables, saying, Behold, a sower went forth to sow;
4. And when he sowed, some seeds fell by the way side, and the fowls came and devoured them up.
5. Some fell upon stony places, where they had not much earth: and forthwith they sprung up, because they had no deepness of earth.
6. And when the sun was up, they were scorched; and because they had no root, they withered away.
7. And some fell among thorns; and the thorns sprung up, and choked them.
8. But other fell into good ground, and brought forth fruit, some an hundredfold, some sixtyfold, some thirtyfold.
9. Who hath ears to hear, let him hear.

► Compare the two versions, verse by verse, pointing out both similarities and differences.

► You may also want to compare the two passages with a twentieth-century translation. The passage is in Matthew 13:1–9.

The next example of Middle English is by Geoffrey Chaucer, the first great English writer. His best-known work is *The Canterbury Tales,* an account of a group of travelers who amused themselves by telling stories as they went on a pilgrimage to Canterbury. The Prologue describes the pilgrims, each portrait filled with more vivid detail than any earlier English writers had included. The portrait we'll look at is that of the Squire, the son of the Knight who is described first.

> With hym ther was his sone, a yong SQUIER,
> A lovyere [*lover*] and a lusty bacheler,[1]
> With lokkes crulle as they were leyd in presse
>   [*curled as if with curling irons*].
> Of twenty yeer of age he was, I gesse.
> Of his stature he was of evene [*moderate*] lengthe,
> And wonderly delyvere [*active*], and of greet
>   strengthe.
> And he hadde been somtyme in chyvachie
>   [*cavalry expeditions*]
> In Flaundres, in Artoys, and Pycardie,
> And born hym weel [*borne himself well*], as of so
>   litel space [*considering the short time*],
> In hope to stonden in his lady grace.
> Embrouded [*Embroidered*] was he, as it were a
>   meede [*meadow*]
> Al ful of fresshe floures, whyte and reede.
> Syngynge he was, or floytynge [*fluting*], al the
>   day;
> He was as fressh as is the month of May.
> Short was his gowne, with sleves longe and wyde.
> Wel koude he sitte on hors and faire ryde.

---

[1]A "bacheler" could be either a bachelor in the modern sense, or a young man aspiring to knighthood. This squire is unmarried, but hardly old enough to be considered a bachelor as the term is used today.

He koude songes make and wel endite [*compose*],
Juste [*Joust*] and eek [*also*] daunce, and weel
    purtreye [*draw*] and write.
So hoote [*hotly*] he lovede that by nyghtertale
    [*at night*]
He sleep namoore than dooth a nyghtyngale.
Curteis he was, lowely [*humble*], and servysable
    [*willing to serve*],
And carf [*carved*] biforn his fader at the table.[2]

▶ In what ways does Chaucer's versification differ from that of *Beowulf* (page 68) and of Layamon (pages 87–88)? Consider rhyme, meter, and alliteration.

▶ Apart from substitutions for certain words such as *chyvachie*, what changes would have to be made in these lines to make them good, everyday Modern English?

▶ If you, Beowulf, and the Squire could be brought together, could you more easily understand the Squire or Beowulf? Could Beowulf more easily understand you or the Squire? Could the Squire more easily understand you or Beowulf? Give specific reasons for your answers.

[2]One of the duties of a squire was to carve the knight's meat.

It should be noted that Middle English had several dialects, and that some of these seem more distant from Modern English than Chaucer does. As a single example, note these lines from *Sir Gawain and the Green Knight*, written in Chaucer's century in the West Midland dialect, which differed in a number of details from Chaucer's East Midland:

> *There tourneyed heroes betimes   full many*
> Þer   tournayed tulkes by-tymez ful mony,
>
> *Jousted full joyously these wellborn*
> Justed   ful jollilé   þyse gentyle knigtes,
>
> *Afterward returned*
> Syþen   kayred   to þe court, caroles to make.

To make even the translated passage into understandable Modern English, we have to change the word order considerably: "In good time many heroes held a tournament there. These wellborn knights jousted very joyously and afterward returned to the court to sing carols."

2. Pronunciation
of Middle English

Middle English is not very different in pronunciation from Old English. Although phonologists have described a considerable number of small changes and have analyzed variations among ME dialects, the major differences are these:

a. One of the OE sounds of *h*, the one like the *ch* in German *ich*, disappeared, so that *h* was pronounced about like Mod E *h*. The *h* sound—and later the letter *h*—was dropped from *hl*, *hn*, and *hr*: OE *hnutu* (nut), for example, was spelled with an *h* and pronounced "hnoo-too" (*oo* as in *foot*); but in Middle English this became *nute*, pronounced "noo-tuh."

b. The voiceless sounds of *f*, *s*, and *th* became more clearly distinguished from the voiced sounds of *v*, *z*, and *th* respectively.

c. Some *w*'s were lost, especially after *s* and *t*. In OE *twā* (two) the *w* was pronounced, but today we don't pronounce the *w* in *two* because it vanished in Middle English. Similarly OE *sweostor* moved in Middle English in the direction of Mod E *sister*.

d. As you may have noticed, the infinitive forms of OE verbs usually ended in *n*, as in *grētan* (to greet). In Middle English this *n* tended to be lost, so that most infinitives ended in the vague "uh" sound: *grēte*, "gray-tuh."

e. OE *ā* was pronounced as in *calm;* in Middle English the pronunciation changed to "aw" as in Mod E *dawn*. The spelling also changed, to *o* or *oo*. Thus OE *hām* (home) became ME *hom* or *hoom*, pronounced "hawm," and OE *stān* (stone) became *ston*, "stawn."

f. OE *æ*, pronounced like the *a* in Mod E *at*, changed temporarily in Middle English to *a* as in *art*, and the written symbol *æ* was replaced by *a*. Later the pronunciation went back to that of *æ*, but the spelling did not. If the ME pronunciation had remained, we would say "aht" and "kaht" for *at* and *cat*.

g. OE *y*, as in *fyllan* (to fill), had a sound like the German *ü* in *dünn* or the French *u* in *tu*. This became simplified in Middle English to the *i* sound as in Mod E *fill*.

h. The pronunciations of OE diphthongs like *ēo* are shown on page 72. In Middle English these became simple vowels (though a new set of diphthongs developed). Thus OE *trēo* (tree), "tray-oh," became ME *tree*, "tray."

The following table[3] indicates the ME pronunciation of vowel sounds:

ME vowels	ME examples	Pronunciations
a	drank	"drahnk"
	shape	"shah-puh"
aa	caas (case)	"kahs"
e	lest	"lest"
	depe (deep)	"day-puh"
	clene (clean)	"klæ-nuh"
		(*æ* as in Mod E *at*)
ee	meel (meal)	"mel"
	feend (fiend)	"faynd"
i	milk	"milk"
	tide	"tee-duh"
ii	wiis (wise)	"weese"
o	god	"gawd"
	over	"aw-ver"
	dom (doom)	"dome"
	good	"goed"
	coppe (cup)	"koop-uh"
		(*oo* as in Mod E *good*)
	wolf	"wolf"
	rode (road)	"raw-duh"
oo	hoom (home)	"hawm"
	hood	"hoed"
	food	"foed"

[3]Adapted from Margaret M. Bryant, *Modern English and Its Heritage*, 2nd ed., New York: The Macmillan Company, 1962, pp. 195–196. Reprinted by permission.

u	us	"oos"
		(*oo* as in Mod E *good*)
	put	"poot"
		(*oo* as in Mod E *good*)
	entuned	"en-tyoon-ed"
		(*oo* as in Mod E *coo*)
y	tyl (till)	"till"
	swyn (swine)	"swin"
ai, ay	dai, day	"dæ-ih"
		(*æ* as in Mod E *at*)
au, aw	sauce, sawce	"sow-suh"
ei, ey	wei, wey	"wæ-ih"
		(*æ* as in Mod E *at*)
eu, ew	deu, dew	"dyoo"
		(*oo* as in Mod E *coo*)
iu, iw	Tiuesnight,	"tyoo-ehs-nikt"
	Tiwesnigkt	(*oo* as in Mod E *coo*)
ou, ow	oure, owre	"oo-ruh"
		(*oo* as in Mod E *coo*)
	oune, owne	"aw-oo-nuh"
		(*oo* as in Mod E *good*)
	sought	"saw-ookt"
		(*oo* as in Mod E *good*)
oi, oy	coine, coyne	"koy-nuh"
er	service	"sehr-vee-suh"
ir	first	"fihrst"
		(*ih* like *i* in *it*)
or	word	"wawrd"
ur	hurt	"hoort"
		(*oo* as in Mod E *good*)

Notice especially that many final *e*'s that are now silent were pronounced in Middle English. See *shape* and *tide,* for instance. People used to think that Chaucer's poetry was metrically irregular, that it did not scan very well. But when linguists discovered that most of the final *e*'s were pronounced, it became clear that Chaucer's versification was much more regular than had been supposed.

▶ Practice the ME pronunciations given in the table. After practicing for a few minutes, you should be able to pronounce fairly accurately most of the ME words in the examples on pages 86-95. Try them. Although some of them may give you trouble and not come out quite the way Chaucer himself would have said them, you should be fairly close to the ME sounds. If in a literature class you come later to selections from Chaucer and his contemporaries, you will have a pretty good idea of what their language sounded like.

Although we won't go into details about ME dialects, the map on page 100 shows the chief dialect areas. The dialects differed somewhat in vocabulary and in grammar, but especially in pronunciation. Some of the differences can be traced back to the fact that Jutes, Angles, and Saxons had settled, centuries before, in different parts of England. Others were due to varying amounts of influence of the Danes and the Normans, and to nearness to the Celts, who had continued to live in Wales, Ireland, and Scotland. Scandinavian influence, for example, is greater in the northern dialects than in the southern.

Middle English Dialects

In the fourteenth century a man named Ranulph Higden described the situation in a Latin work called *Polychronicon*. Here is a translation of part of what he said:

> Men of eastern England and men of western England sound more alike than do northerners and southerners. For that reason the Mercians, who live in middle England, can better understand the side languages, northern and southern, than northern and southern can understand each other. All the language of the northerners, and especially that of York, is so sharp, slitting, and rasping, and unshaped, that we southern men can hardly understand it at all.

The Southeast Midland dialect is of special interest to us, because it is from this dialect that present-day standard English developed. London, you will note, is in this area, though very close to Kent. Although it was only a small city in ME times, it was the center of culture and of government. Most of the great ME writers—Chaucer, for example, and Wycliffe and Gower—lived in London, and after Caxton brought printing to the British Isles, the city was also a center for printers. For these reasons, the London brand of Southeast Midland dialect became the one that many speakers throughout the nation tried to imitate. So, in later years, did many other people across the Atlantic in North America.

However, language never remains the same for very long. In London itself, near the end of the ME period, the language of the court and of other well-educated persons gradually became somewhat different from that of the "lower classes," as the British called them. The Cockney dialect, used by many but not all the people in these lower classes, was beginning to develop in the year 1500, and is today spoken by many Londoners and by some of their cousins in Australia and in other parts of the world.

3. Middle English Grammar

Loss of inflections. You will recall that OE nouns, verbs, and adjectives had many inflectional endings. Partly because of the Danish and Norman invasions, and partly for other reasons, the number of these endings gradually decreased throughout much of the ME period. Often the ending first changed to an -*en* and then to an -*e* (pronounced with the schwa sound, "uh"), and then disappeared entirely.

Nouns. Because of the loss of inflectional endings, the ME noun forms became much like those we use today (except, of course, in pronunciation). Thus *ston* was the singular form for all purposes except to show possession, when *stones* was used. (The apostrophe we use in the possessive forms was a later invention.) There was only one plural form, *stones*. Some *n* plurals still existed, though, such as *shoon* (shoes).

Pronouns. The dual number of the personal pronouns disappeared by the thirteenth century. It may have been a rather convenient form to have, but apparently not enough people thought so to keep using it. Late Middle English and Modern English, therefore, have only singular and plural personal pronoun forms.

For the first person, *I*, *ich*, and *ik* were all found in Middle English, but today only *I* remains. *Me* was the objective form, as in Old English, and *we* and *us* continued as the plurals. *My* began to be used as a genitive, though *min* and *mine* were also common, especially before vowel sounds. The genitive plural was variously spelled *ure*, *urne*, *oure*, and *ourne*.

Something rather interesting happened to the second-person pronouns. In Old English *þū* (thou), *þīn* (thine), and *þē* (thee) were singular, and *gē* (ye), *ēower* (your), and *ēow* (you) were plural. During the fourteenth century, however, it became polite to use the plural forms of *ye* in addressing just one person, especially someone who was highly respected. The forms of *thou,* including *thy* or *thine* and *thee* (all spelled in several ways in Middle English), were used in talking with a member of the family, an inferior, or a close friend. No doubt this custom was influenced by the French language, which still uses the plural form *vous* as a mark of respect and the singular *tu* as a sign of familiarity.

The third-person singular masculine pronouns remained *he, his, him*. The feminine forms were more fickle, though. *She* began to be used, but *he, heo,* and *hie* were still found. The genitive was usually *hire* or *here,* but *he, ho,* or *hie* was the accusative. A dative *hire* was probably the ancestor of Mod E *her.* For the neuter, *hit* and *it* were fighting it out, and *his* or sometimes *it* was used as the genitive, since *its* had not yet been invented. The third-person plurals included *they* or *thei,* but *hem* rather than *them.* The plural genitive was *hire* or *here,* shortened from OE *hiera* or *heora*.

Adjectives. Adjectives were tremendously simplified in Middle English. Instead of having to select from a large number of different endings, as in Old English, a speaker of Middle English needed to choose from only two. For example, after *the* or a word like *this, that, my, his,* but only in the singular, the ME spelling of *good* was *god;* in all other instances it was *gode.* The sound of the final *e* was gradually lost, however, so that finally only *god* (now *good*) remained. By late Middle English other adjectives followed the same pattern, merging into the single form that makes present-day adjectives so easy to use that even foreigners have little trouble.

Verbs. Verbs were also simplified in Middle English, though less so than adjectives. You will recall that Old English had many "strong" verbs that were the ancestors of most of today's "irregular" verbs—*drink, sing,* and *freeze,* for example. In Middle English about a third of the strong verbs either disappeared from the language or became "weak" (regular) in form. Among those that became weak in Middle English or a little later were *bark, burn, braid, carve, climb, flow, help, melt, mourn, starve, swallow, swell, yell, yelp,* and *yield.* When we say "*molten* metal," we are using a remnant of the old strong form, and if you hear someone say that his arm "*swoll* up," that word too goes back many centuries. Our verb *swell,* in fact, went only part way toward complete "weakness": it has the weak past tense *swelled,* but the past participle may be either the weak *swelled* or the strong *swollen.*

The *-an* and *-on* endings of many OE verbs in ME times changed first to *-en.* Then the *n* started to drop away, and in late Middle English and early Modern

English the *e* also gradually disappeared. Let's look at *bind* as an example:

OE	ME	Mod E
bindan (inf.)	binden, *then* binde	bind
bundon (p.t.)	bounden, *then* bounde	bound
bunden (p.p.)	bounden, *then* bounde	bound

The personal endings of verbs still showed some differences from Modern English forms. For example:

PRESENT
{ I binde — we, you, they binden
thou bindest (*later* binde)
he bindeth }

PAST
{ I bounden (*later* bounde) — we, you, they
thou bounde — bounden (*later*
he bounden (*later* bounde) — bounde) }

The verb *bēon* (to be) had not yet settled down in Middle English and appeared in various forms, of which these are most typical:

PRESENT
{ I am — we, you, they bee *or*
thou art *or* beest — been *or* sinden *or*
he is *or* beeth — ar(e)n }

PAST
{ I was — we, you, they were(n)
thou wast *or* were
he was }

One form of *will* was *wol* or *woll* or *wolle*. This survives in our contraction *won't* (= *woll not*). If language were consistent, and if ME *woll* had not existed, we would be saying *win't*.

One more small point. In Middle English, when you encounter *can* or *could* (perhaps spelled differently), the meaning intended is "know how to" and "knew how to." Since a person who knows how to do something is usually able to do it, the modern meanings of "can" and "could" developed.

► Examine the verbs in the examples of Middle English on pages 86–95 and note to what extent they conform to what has just been said, or vary from it. (During a time of considerable language change, especially when different dialects may be involved, no great consistency can be expected.)

Adverbs. The process of change from OE adverbial forms like *eornostlīce* to *eornostly* (earnestly) went on in Middle English. And in this period also, the *e* sound in OE adverbs ending in *-e* generally dropped out. For example, in Old English, *heard* (hard) was an adjective; *hearde* was the adverbial form. In Middle English these came together as *hard,* so that today we may refer to a *hard* ball (adjective) or say that someone worked *hard* (adverb), using the same form for both. Similarly, OE *slāwe* was an adverb, which became our *slow,* as in "Drive *slow*." This usage has been attacked as "incorrect" by people who do not know the history of their language; it was correct in Middle English and has remained so. *Slow*, like *hard,* *fast, first,* and *wide* (as in "The boat swung *wide*"), is perfectly acceptable as an adverb.

Some other Mod E adverbs that seem a little strange go back to OE or ME genitives. For instance, *once* and *twice* come from the genitive (possessive) of *one* and *two,* so that literally they mean "of the one" and "of the two." Other survivors of old genitives are *sideways, backwards, northwards, homewards,* and *nights* (as in "He works *nights*"). For some of these words, an alternative form without the *s* has come into being; we are more likely, for instance, to hear *northward* than *northwards.*

▶ What other examples of adverbs like *hard* can you think of that are identical with adjectives? What other examples of adverbs like *once, sideways, backwards,* and *nights*?

5

the Language of shakespeare

1. Some Examples
of Early Modern English

THE years from about 1500 to about 1700 A.D. make up the Early Modern English period *(E Mod E)*. You will find that the examples you will look at are considerably easier to read than the earlier ones, because they are quite similar to the English of today. You will also find, though, that they still retain some of the characteristics of Middle English.

The first selection is from a once very popular book called *Herball*, which was a sort of guide to homemade medicines that could be made from herbs, and which was crammed with false information. The 1525 title page says that the book was

imprynted by me Richard Banckes, dwellynge in London, a lytel fro yᵉ Stockes in yᵉ Pultry,

y^e .xxv. day of Marche. The yere of our lorde
.M.ccccc. & xxv.[1]

Besides the interesting reminder that London had no
street addresses in those days and that "stockes"
for exhibiting prisoners stood in the streets, the title
page has a number of items of linguistic interest to
observe.

► What is some evidence that *y* and *i* were used almost interchangeably? Which words show the survival
of the final *e* of Chaucer's day (although by 1525 it was
not usually pronounced)? What other E Mod E spellings in these lines differ from Late Modern English
(L Mod E)?

The spelling *y^e* for *the* in the *Herball* title page is of
special interest. You recall that *þ* (the thorn) was used
in Old English and often in Middle English for the
th sound. ME scribes sometimes wrote the thorn in a
shape somewhat like that of *y*, but the pronunciation
was still that of *th*. *Y^e* and *y^t* were often used as abbreviations for *the* and *that*, but the words were not
pronounced "ye" and "yat." (If you see a modern

[1]This statement and the following selection from *Herball* are taken from
Thomas Pyles, *The Origins and Development of the English Language*,
New York: Harcourt Brace Jovanovich, 1964, pp. 168–170. Only two copies
of *Herball* are known to exist, even though the book went through fifteen
or more editions.

sign like "Ye Olde Antique Shoppe" and hear somebody say "ye" instead of "the," you may feel faintly amused and superior, because now you know better!)

One part of *Herball* tells of the supposed marvelous qualities of the herb called *rosemary:*

This herbe is hote and dry, take the flowres and put them in a lynen clothe, & so boyle them in fayre clene water to ye halfe & coole it & drynke it, for it is moche worth agaynst all euylles in the body. Also take the flowres & make powder therof and bynde it to the ryght arme in a lynen clothe, and it shall make the lyght and mery. Also ete the flowres with hony fastynge with sowre breed and there shall ryse in the none euyll swellynges. . . . Also take the leues & put thē into a vessel of wyne and it shall preserue ye wyne fro tartnesse & euyl sauour, and yf thou sell that wyne, thou shall haue good lucke & spede in the sale. . . . Also yf thou haue the coughe, drynke the water of the leues boyled in whyte wyne, & thou shalbe hole. Also take the rynde of Rosemary & make powder therof and drynke it for the pose [*head cold*], & thou shalbe delyuered therof. . . . Also put therof in thy doores or in thy howse & thou shalbe without daunger of Adders and other venymous serpentes.

▶ Reread the selection above and try to answer these questions:

1. What does *thē* mean in line 11? What does *the* mean in lines 7 and 9?

2. What evidence is there that the writer was not consistent in using abbreviations?

3. List at least ten of the words in which Banckes used a *y* where Late Modern English uses *i*.

4. What are some examples of *u* instead of present-day *v*? (*V* did not enter our language until ME times. For a while *v* and *u* were used interchangeably. Then *v* came to be generally used at the beginning of words, *u* elsewhere, even though in words like *haue* the *u* had what we would call a *v* sound. By the seventeenth century *v* was used for a consonant sound and *u* for a vowel sound, as is true today.)

5. What do the words *sowre* and *howse* show about E Mod E spelling?

6. In line 12, what does *fro* mean? This spelling goes back to the Scandinavian word *frā*, which had no *m*. It survives even today in the expression "to and ___?___ ."

7. What two words are used instead of *you*?

8. Notice the words "thou shall haue good lucke & spede in the sale." This is the same kind of "speed" found at least as late as the nineteenth century in expressions like "I wish you good speed." What do you guess it means? Check your guess in a dictionary: look for a definition of *speed* that is labeled *Archaic* or something similar.

9. Why do you suppose that *shalbe* (and its possible partner *wilbe*) did not remain in the language?

10. In line 16, *whole* is spelled *hole*. In Old English it was *hāl* and in Middle English

hole. Try to guess why and how the modern spelling with *w* developed.

The next selection, although it was written a quarter of a century or so later than the first one, is somewhat more difficult to read. The reason is that it is written in a southwestern dialect instead of the London dialect. This southwestern dialect became the usual one in stage plays with uneducated rural characters; some of Shakespeare's country folk speak similarly.

The selection is from a popular comedy of uncertain authorship, called *Gammer Gurton's Needle. Gammer* means "old lady"; it is a contracted form of *godmor* (godmother), just as *gaffer* (old man) is contracted from *godfar* (godfather). The plot is a very slight one about the excitement and quarrels that arose when Gammer Gurton lost her needle while mending the trousers of her servant, Hodge. In this scene, from the early part of the play, Hodge is talking with the mischief-making Diccon.

HODGE. See! so cham [*I am*] arayed with
      dablynge in the durt!
She that set me to ditchinge, ich wold [*I wish*] she
      had the squrt [*diarrhea*]!
Was neuer poore soule that such a life had!
Gogs [*God's*] bones, thys vylthy glaye [*clay*]
      hase drest mee to bad!
Gods soule, see how this stuff teares!
      (*Hodge examines the tears in his breeches.*)
Iche were better to bee a bearward [*bearkeeper*]
      and set to keepe beares!

By the masse, here is a gasshe! a shamefull hole
   in-deade!
An [*If*] one stytch teare furder, a man may thruste
   in his heade.

  DICCON. By my fathers soule, Hodge, if I
   shulde now be sworne,
I can not chuse but say thy breech is foule be-
   torne!
But the next remedye in such a case and hap
   [*happenstance*]
Is to plaunche [*place* or *plop*] on a piece as brode
   as thy cap.

  HODGE. Gogs soule, man, tis not yet two
   dayes fully ended
Synce my dame Gurton, chem [*I am*] sure, these
   breches amended!
But cham made such a drudge, to trudge at euery
   neede,
Chwold [*I would*] rend it though it were stitched
   wath sturdy pacthreede.

► You may remember that in Old English the word
for *I* was *ic*, generally pronounced about like German
Ich, but sometimes about like Mod E *itch*. How is that
fact probably related to Hodge's use of *cham* and
several other words?

► What is the present form of *vylthy* (line 4)? Remember that *v* is a voiced sound and that *f* is the cor-

responding unvoiced sound. Hodge's dialect, then, sometimes uses a voiced sound where the standard English of today uses an unvoiced one. Find a different example of this fact in the same line.

▶ In line 8, Hodge says *furder* where today's standard English speaker would say what word? Another example is OE *fadir,* which today is what word? How are the pronunciations "dis," "dat," and "dem," sometimes heard today, related to these examples?

▶ In line 14, Hodge says *amended* where today we would use what word? In a dictionary look up the derivations of *amend, emend,* and *mend* to see whether the three words are related. What do you find about *mend* that shows that *amend* is an older word?

▶ If the last word of the selection puzzles you, look up *packthread* in your dictionary.

We'll next look at a bit of Sir Philip Sidney's *An Apologie for Poetry,* written about 1580 and published in 1595.

Sith then Poetrie is of all humane learning the most auncient, and of most fatherly antiquitie, as from whence other learnings have taken theyr beginnings: sith it is so universall, that no learned Nation dooth despise it, nor no barbarous Nation is without it: sith both Roman and Greek gave divine names unto it: the one of prophecying, the other of making. . . . Sith neither his [the poet's] description, nor his ende, contayneth any evill, the thing described cannot be evill: Sith his effects be so good as to teach goodnes and to delight the learners. . . . Sith all his kindes are not onlie in their united formes, but in their severed dissections fully commendable, I think, (and I think I thinke rightly) the Lawrell crowne appointed for tryumphing Captaines, doth worthilie (of al other learnings) honor the Poets tryumph.

Note Sidney's liking for the long sentence. The sixteenth century (and still more the seventeenth) was moving toward longer sentences in writing.

If you look at Sidney's spellings and compare them with the spellings in the earlier selections, you will observe that many of Sidney's appear more modern; he has *e*'s at the end of fewer words, for one thing. By the time Sidney's work was published, the English had been printing books for about a century, and printers had gradually standardized spelling, even though they were not consistent in using *y* rather than *ie* at the end of a word, and even though, as in this selection, they might spell a word like *think* in two different ways in the same sentence.

The word *sith* (now *since*) is an interesting survival. An OE word that meant "then" was *siððan*. An *es* was sometimes added to it, with a change of meaning to something like "after then" or "after that time." In

Middle English this became *sithence* or *sithenes,* which was shortened in at least four ways. One was *sith;* another was our word *since,* which dates back to about 1450; a third was *sin,* earlier *sinnes;* and a fourth was *syne,* as in "Auld Lang Syne." All four of these were available to Sidney, but on this occasion, at least, he chose *sith.*

You may recall that during the Renaissance (the fourteenth through the sixteenth centuries) there was tremendous interest in the literature, language, art, and general culture of the ancient Greeks and Romans. One result was the borrowing of many words, especially from Latin. Frequently the borrowing was from French, which had taken the words from Latin. In the following passage from John Lyly's *Euphues and His England,* published in 1581, words that can be traced back to Latin are italicized. Lyly is here praising his queen, Elizabeth I.

> Two and twenty years hath she borne the sword with such *justice,* that neither *offenders* could *complain* of *rigor,* nor the *innocent* of wrong; yet so *tempered* with *mercy* as *malefactors* have been sometimes *pardoned* upon hope of *grace,* and the *injured requited* to *ease* their grief, insomuch that in the whole *course* of her *glorious reign,* it could never be said that either the *poor* were *oppressed* without *remedy,* or the guilty *repressed* without *cause,* bearing this engraven in her *noble* heart, that *justice* without *mercy* were *extreme injury,* and *pity* without *equity plain partiality,* and that it is as great *tyranny* not to *mitigate* laws, as *iniquity* to break them.

► There are 112 words in the Lyly passage. What proportion of the words are of Latin origin?

► Compare the other words with those derived from Latin. In general, are the Latin words longer or shorter? Are they generally more common or less common words?

Not everyone during this period, however, liked the idea of borrowing words from Latin and other languages. Some people argued that English should be kept "pure." A man named Sir John Cheke, for instance, in about 1550 translated part of the New Testament into "purely Anglo-Saxon" words. The great poet Edmund Spenser also favored avoiding Latinisms, although he found he could not get along without them. The following lines are one stanza of his *Faerie Queene* (1590), an extremely long poem describing the adventures of knights who represented various good qualities. In this stanza, one of these knights has been taken to the small dwelling of a hermit.

A little lowly hermitage it was,
Downe in a dale, hard by a forests side,
Far from resort of people that did pas
In traveill to and froe: a little wyde [*a short
distance away*]
There was an holy chapell edifyde [*built*],

Wherein the hermite dewly wont to say
His holy thinges each morne and eventyde:
Thereby a christall streame did gently play,
Which from a sacred fountaine welled forth alway.

▶ Of the 66 words in the Spenser stanza, the following can be traced to Latin: *hermitage, forest, people, traveill, chapell, edifyde, hermite, dewly* (duly), *christall* (crystal), *gently, sacred, fountaine.* Is the proportion of Latin-based words smaller or greater than in the passage from Lyly? According to your dictionary, which of these words came into English from Latin by way of French? How can you account for the fact that so many of our words came in along this route?

▶ What conclusions can you draw from the fact that Spenser, who preferred "pure English" words, nevertheless used many that had come from Latin?

We'll look now at some scattered lines from Act I of William Shakespeare's *Macbeth* (1606) to note some other features of the language as it was developing in Early Modern English. (It will be useful if you have a copy of *Macbeth* handy for this discussion.)

A battle was going on in verb forms, especially in the present tense. Here are a few examples:

He can report,
As *seemeth* by his plight, of the revolt
The newest state. (Act I, Scene ii, lines 1–3)

not certain if proverb or verb form

So should he look
That *seems* to speak things strange. (I, ii, 46–47)

↗ more modern

Who *comes* here? (I, ii, 44)

Whence *camest* thou, worthy Thane? (I, ii, 48)

Thus must thou do, if thou *have* it. (I, v, 24)

Where *hast* thou been, Sister? (I, iii, 1)

What he *hath* lost, noble Macbeth *hath* won. (I, ii, 67)

These lines show that verbs ending in *-est* and *-eth* were battling it out with the simpler forms like *seem* and *seems*. The *-est* and *-eth* forms were survivors of the OE inflectional endings that gradually were lost.

► If you turn to a copy of *Macbeth*, you can find in the first act or elsewhere many more of the older forms, such as *doth, hadst,* and *shalt,* often side by side with present-day forms. If each member of the class examines carefully the verbs in a different set of ten or fifteen lines, the class can draw some interesting conclusions about the details of the verb battle.

The struggle between *thou (thee, thy, thine)* and *you (your, yours)* is also illustrated in the first act of *Macbeth.* You will recall that *thou (thee, thy, thine)* was generally used in addressing inferiors, friends, or members of the family, and that *you (your, yours)* or sometimes *ye* was the usual form for addressing superiors or strangers. Most of the following examples follow those principles:

[Prince Malcolm, to a sergeant]
Say to the King the knowledge of the broil
As thou didst leave it.   (I, ii, 6–7)

[One witch to another]
Where hast thou been, Sister?   (I, iii, 1)

[Ross, a nobleman, to Macbeth, who is also a nobleman]
The king hath happily received, Macbeth,
The news of thy success. And when he reads
Thy personal venture in the rebels' fight . . .
   (I, iii, 89–91)

[King Duncan to Macbeth]
                    Thou art so far before
That swiftest wing of recompense is slow
To overtake thee.   (I, iv, 16–18)

[Macbeth to King Duncan]
The rest is labour, which is not used for you.
I'll be myself the harbinger [*messenger*] and
   make joyful
The hearing of my wife with your approach.
   (I, iv, 44–46)

[Lady Macbeth to Macbeth]
                        Was the hope drunk
   Wherein you dressed yourself? Hath it slept
      since?
   And wakes it now, to look so green and pale
   At what it did so freely? From this time
   Such I account thy love. Art thou afeard
   To be the same in thine own act and valor
   As thou art in desire?   (I, vii, 35–41)

► In which of the above quotations is the usual pattern of address not followed?

In Early Modern English questions were phrased
differently from the way we word them today, as
these quotations from *Macbeth* show:

                        Dismay'd not this
   Our captains, Macbeth and Banquo?   (I, ii, 33–
      34)

                        Live you?   (I, iii, 42)

   Whence camest thou, worthy Thane?   (I, ii, 48)

   Went it not so?   (I, iii, 87)

   MACBETH.
                        My dearest love,
   Duncan comes here tonight.
   LADY MACBETH.
                        And when goes hence?

   (I, v, 58–60)

► How would we say each of the questions in the above quotations?

Interestingly, the modern form of questions with *do* or *did* was also in existence in Shakespeare's day, as these quotations show:

Good sir, why do you start, and seem to fear?
(I, iii, 51)

                       Why do you dress me
In borrow'd robes? (I, iii, 108–109)

Do you not hope your children shall be kings?
(I, iii, 118)

Today we always use *do* or *did* in questions like those in the eight examples above. For instance, we always say "Did he go away?"—not "Went he away?" In Shakespeare's time, although both question patterns were used, the "Went he away?" form was by far the more frequent.

Something similar is true of negatives. Today, for example, we make a negative of "I know him" by using *do* and *not:* "I do not know him." The past tense "I knew him" is made negative with *did, not,* and *know:* "I did not know him." In Elizabethan times, however, although the pattern with *do* and *did* existed, usually only *not* was added: "I know him not." "I know not the answer." "I knew him not." "I knew not whence he came." On the following page are some examples from *Macbeth*.

> To me you speak not.   (I, iii, 57)

> Whether he was combined
> With those of Norway, or did line [*support*] the
>   rebel
> With hidden help and vantage [*assistance*], or
>   that with both
> He labor'd in his country's wrack, I know not.
>   (I, iii, 111-114)

>   . . . to be king
> Stands not within the prospect of belief.   (I, iii,
>   73-74)

► Tell how each of the above negative sentences
would be expressed today.

2. Pronunciation
of Early Modern English

Between 1400 and 1650 or 1700, a number of English vowels changed greatly in pronunciation. If this "Great Vowel Shift" had not occurred, our "long" vowels today would sound much more like those of Italian, Spanish, and other Continental languages, and also, of course, much more like ME vowels.

Not all the changes were completed by Shakespeare's time (1564-1616). His pronunciations were often apparently somewhere between those of Middle

English and those of today. For simplicity, though, we'll look only at what the ME long vowels eventually became.

In Middle English the *a* in words like *name* and *place* sounded like "ah": "nah-muh" and "plah-suh." Now we use an "ay" sound that is really a diphthong (two vowel sounds pronounced together). You can hear this for yourself if you say "ay" slowly.

In Middle English it was the *e* that had an "ay" sound: *swete* (or *sweete*) was "sway-tuh," and *grete* was "gray-tuh." Today these words are *sweet* and *greet*, with what we usually call a long-*e* sound.

In Middle English the *i* in *child* or *bite* was pronounced with this long-*e* sound: "cheeld" and "bee-tuh." Now it has what we call a long-*i* sound (as in *ice*), which is actually another diphthong.

Perhaps you recall that OE *hām* and *stān* changed from an "ah" sound to an "aw" sound in Middle English: "hawm" and "stawn." During the Great Vowel Shift a further change occurred, to the long-*o* sound of the modern *home* and *stone*.

Words that had a long-*o* sound in Middle English, however, changed to the "oo" sound of *moon*. Thus ME *mone* "mo-nuh" is today's "moon," and ME *ro(o)te* "ro-tuh" is today's "root" (as pronounced by those people who rhyme it with *hoot* and *toot*). In some words this *oo* sound has been shortened, as in *book, foot, good,* and *look*.

ME *hūs* and *mūs* both rhymed with modern *goose;* that is, both had the "oo" sound of *loose* and *moose*. Such words are now pronounced with an "ow" sound: *house* and *mouse*.

There were some other vowel changes too, but these are the most important ones. You should now be able to answer the following questions.

► Before the Great Vowel Shift, how were these words pronounced? *green* (ME *grene*), *how* (ME *hu*), *ice* (ME *is*), *fire* (ME *fyr* or *fyre*), *fiend* (ME *feend*), *doom* (ME *dom*), *keen* (ME *cene*), *out* (ME *ut*), *cool* (ME *col*), *bone* (ME *ban*), *boat* (ME *bot* or *bote*).

► Turn to the list on pages 97–98, showing ME pronunciations. How is each example word pronounced today? About how many are exactly the same?

Nobody knows precisely why the Great Vowel Shift occurred. After his description of the various shifts in sounds, Professor L. M. Myers comments:

> . . . The whole process sounds most unlikely, especially the last part. Nobody knows why it happened, so there is no use worrying about that. We have very convincing evidence that it somehow did, and at least it explains one of the main peculiarities in English spelling.[2]

Changes in consonant sounds in Early Modern English were not numerous. But one of these changes explains why we use the same two letters—*gh*—in spelling two words as different in sound as *rough* and *though*. Previously this *gh* was used to indicate a sort of *k* sound, like the *ch* in German *Ich*. Thus *night* (also spelled *niht*) sounded something like "nikt." In Early Modern English, however, this *k* sound changed, becoming either an *f* sound, as in modern

---

[2]Myers, *op. cit.*, p. 168.

126

rough and *cough*, or becoming silent, as in modern *though* and *thought*.

► Try to think of other modern words in which the *gh* indicates an *f* sound or is silent.

We have already noticed (page 115) that *d* and *th* were battling it out in words like *furder—further* and *fadir—father*. Shakespeare sometimes wrote *murder*, sometimes *murther*. Other examples are *moder—mother* and *burthen—burden*. As you see, sometimes the *d* won and sometimes the *th*.

Today we sometimes use a *y* sound in words ending in *-ial* or *-ious*, such as *genial* and *bilious*. But in Early Modern English, the *i* had the sound of the *i* in *it:* "bil-i-us," for example.

There was confusion in Early Modern English about words ending in *n*. Sometimes where Middle English had a *d* sound after the *n,* the *d* sound was dropped; thus ME *laund* became modern *lawn*, and *swound* finally became our *swoon*. But at other times a *d* sound was added. The word *sound* itself was *soun* in Middle English, and our word *lend* was *lene*.

In case you have ever wondered why we spell *talk, half, calf, salve,* and *folk* with an *l* in each, the explanation is that these *l*'s were once pronounced, but in Early Modern English, people began to drop them. Our spellings just have not caught up with the change in pronunciation. On the other hand, *fault* used to be *faut* or *faute*, and *falcon* was *faucen*—all without the letter *l*. Then Renaissance scholars decided that since the Latin ancestors of these words contained *l*'s, there should also be *l*'s in the English spellings. So *fault* and *falcon* (and also *vault* instead of the earlier *vaut*) began to appear in print. Even more amusing, two or three centuries later language scholars were hotly debating about the matter, some of them declaring that it was "wrong" to leave out the *l* sounds in pronouncing these words, since doing so obscured their ancestry!

Notice how you pronounce the second half of *nature* and of *leisure*. In Early Modern English the *-ure* was pronounced like the *er* in *her,* and no *ch* or *zh* sound was used, so *nature* was "nay-ter" and *leisure* was "lee-zer." The modern pronunciations of these and other *-ure* words did not become common until the early nineteenth century.

Today many speakers are quite careful about pronouncing the final *ing* in words like *nothing* and *running.* In Shakespeare's time, however, such an *ing* was usually pronounced like *in,* and this continued to be true until about the nineteenth century. In the eighteenth century, for instance, Jonathan Swift rhymed *bliss in* with *missing.* Today probably more persons say "noth'n" and "run'n" than say "nuthing" and "run-ing," though at least in formal speech, careful speakers generally pronounce the *ing* rather distinctly.

3. Vocabulary Growth

According to estimates by certain scholars, there were about 35,000 words in Old English and 45,000 words by 1475. Between 1475 and 1700 the vocabulary grew to about 125,000 words—almost a threefold increase.

Much of this growth was due to the Renaissance interest in Latin and Greek. However, during this period the English explored around the world and many Englishmen traveled on the Continent. Professor Robert A. Peters gives these examples of the borrowings that resulted:

> German *zinc*, Italian *piano*, Spanish *tornado*, Portuguese *flamingo*, Arabic *sofa*, Persian *jasmin*, Dravidian *calico* [from the city of Calicut, India], Javanese *bantam* [from Bantam, Java, from which the fowl are imported], Japanese *kimono*, Malayan *bamboo*, and so on.[3]

Often such borrowings were at second or third hand. For instance, the English took *jasmin* from the French *jasmin* in the sixteenth century. But the French had borrowed the word some time before from the Arabic *yāsmīn*. And the Arabs had previously borrowed it from the Persians. It would be possible, therefore, to say that the English word was borrowed from the French, or from the Arabs, or from the Persians. And if we could trace the Old Persian word back further, we might even find that it had been borrowed from still somebody else.

Of the words taken from Latin, many were never frequently used and have dropped out of the language: *devulgate*, for instance, which meant "to disclose"; *contiguate*, which meant "to be next to"; and *adminiculation*, a jawbreaker that you might revive if ever you need a five-dollar word for "help."

---

[3]Robert A. Peters, *A Linguistic History of English*, Boston: Houghton Mifflin Company, 1968, p. 268.

Thousands of Latin borrowings, though, have remained in the language and today are so commonly used that nobody ever thinks of them as once being foreign. Examples are *education, celebrate, refine, scientific, savage, mature, industry, exist, admiration,* and *generator.*

Latin endings also affected English. Today many English verbs end in *-ate,* like *create* or *dedicate.* Most of these are based on Latin verb forms with the ending *-atus,* like *creatus* and *dedicatus.* Our nouns ending in *-ance, -ence, -ancy,* or *-ency* are almost all based on Latin words that ended in *-antia* or *-entia;* you will have no difficulty in figuring out what English words have come from *constantia* and *confidentia.* The endings *-able* and *-ible* come from Latin *-abilis* and *-ibilis,* meaning "capable or worthy of (being something)"; *memorable,* for example, is from *memorabilis.* Our *-ous* ending, which appears in countless words to show that they are adjectives, is from Latin *-osus* or *-us.*

The Greek language made fewer contributions to English, and some of those came by way of Latin—*climax, crisis, drama, emphasis,* and *system,* for instance. *Machine* and *ode* came from Greek through Latin and French. A number of our words starting with *auto-, bio-,* and *epi-* were borrowed directly from Greek either at this time or later.

French continued to feed words into our language. As you may remember, French began as a dialect of Latin. It is not surprising, therefore, that many of our borrowings from French are second-hand Latin. For example, we took from French many such common words as *marry, air, large, change, poor,* and *pay,* all of which were French adaptations of Latin words. Some of the French words we have borrowed,

130

though, go back to other sources. Our *soup* (from French *soupe*) is of Germanic origin; *picnic* (from French *piquenique*) may also be Germanic but may be a French coinage; *brunette* is a French cognate of the Germanic word for *brown*. As these examples show, languages become infinitely mixed as the centuries pass.

The result of so much borrowing was a great enrichment of the English language. If you look at a thesaurus or a dictionary of synonyms, you will discover that English often has a dozen or more words that mean almost the same thing—almost but not quite. Because of the slight differences, a careful user of words can generally find in English the word that will express the exact shade of meaning he has in mind. For example, if you ever unkindly wanted to refer to someone as a fool, Roget's *Thesaurus* offers you a choice of 109 words! With so many words available, a user of English can generally find the one that communicates exactly what he wants to say. And with so many "exact" words available, he can usually communicate his message briefly and directly.

▶ You will find it interesting to use your dictionary to discover which language or languages gave us each of the words in the following list. You will find that many of the words entered English indirectly; for example, *chocolate* came through Spanish from an Aztec Indian language called Nahuatl. A few of the words in the list were borrowed earlier or later than the E Mod E period. Words marked with an asterisk have especially interesting derivations. (Your class may be asked to divide the responsibility of looking up all the words in the list.)

*admiral	curry (n.)	Satan
*alcohol	*elixir	*seersucker
*algebra	frankfurter	*Seltzer
amber	frolic	*sherry
amen	*gin	*shibboleth
anchovy	gondola	*soprano
area	gradual	soy
armadillo	hamburger	spool
artichoke	hamster	stanza
*autobiography	hoodoo	*suburban
balcony	(cf. voodoo)	superior
ballot	horde	taboo
banana	imitate	*tattoo
baton	*influenza	telephone
bazaar	*intelligentsia	*television
blitzkrieg	kangaroo	tempo
blonde	*khaki	tiger
*carouse	kibitzer	transition
cartoon	landscape	trio
*champagne	*magazine	*tulip
chess	mammoth	tycoon
chlorine	medium	urge
*church	noodle	vindicate
cigarette	opera	waltz
*cipher	*pajamas	wiener
(cf. zero)	*pal	xylophone
cobalt	phenomenon	*yacht
*coffee	polka	*yam
(cf. café)	poodle	
comedy	pretzel	
*cork	quartz	
cot (a bed)	rug	

4. The Grammar
of Early Modern English

On pages 120-124 we noted some of the characteristics of Shakespeare's grammar, such as the frequent use of verb forms like *seemeth* and *didst,* the battle between *thou* and *you,* and the questions and negatives in which *do* or *did* was used less regularly than in Late Modern English *(L Mod E).* Now we'll take a quick look at some other features of E Mod E grammar.

In Old English and to some extent in Middle English, sentences were usually simple or compound. In Early Modern English, though, complex sentences became more frequent. For example, in Middle English a sentence might read "I met a man, and he was the brother of John," but in Early Modern English the same details might be expressed by "I met a man who was the brother of John."

The almost complete loss of inflectional endings made it necessary to work prepositions somewhat harder. In Old English people could say *mannum,* but when the ending disappeared, they had to say *to the men* instead. The prepositions in Early Modern English were generally used as we use them today, but there were some exceptions. Thomas Pyles has collected a few from Shakespeare that sound strange to our ears:

> . . . looke *on* the divell [*devil*]   (*Othello,* II, i, 229)

> He came *of* an errand to mee.   (*Merry Wives,* I, iv, 80)

. . . we are such stuffe/As dreames are made *on*. (*The Tempest,* IV, i, 156–157)

. . . our armies joyn not *in* a hot day (*2 Henry IV,* I, ii, 234)

▶ What would we say instead of each of the above Shakespeare expressions?

The double or multiple negative, as in Shakespeare's "*nor* understood *none neither,*" was very common in Middle English, but less so in Early Modern English, though it still existed. There was also a double superlative, the most famous example of which is Shakespeare's "*most* unkind*est* cut." A double comparative, such as "*more* great*er,*" also could be found. Adjective forms like *beautifulest* and *perfectest* were not uncommon; today we would say "most beautiful" and would either say "most nearly perfect" or "most perfect" or else refuse to compare *perfect* at all, on the ground that if something is perfect, nothing else can be more so. On the other hand, Shakespeare and his contemporaries almost habitually wrote *more close, most dear,* etc., where we more frequently write *closer, dearest,* etc. In their speech and ours, however, both forms appear, not exclusively one.

An especially important development in adjectives was the completion of the trend toward a single form (except for comparison). You remember that in Old English each adjective had a large number of forms; most of these were lost in Middle English, and in Early Modern English only a single form remained. For that reason, when today we use a word like *small* or *pretty*, we never have to worry about finding the right ending.

Anyone who reads a Shakespeare play notices forms of *be* that are no longer used. In the quotations on pages 121–122 you probably saw "thou *art*." For the past tense, *were* was used, but also *wast*, *wert*, and sometimes even *werst*. The form *beest* was also used in expressions like "If thou beest my friend."

Other verbs also seem strange to us. In Early Modern English we find both *spoke* and *spake* as a past tense, both *got* and *gat*, *broke* and *brake*, *drove* and *drave*, *burst* and *brast*. In *Macbeth*, King Duncan says, ". . . his great love, sharp as his spur, hath *holp* him / To his home before us" (I, vi, 23). *Stroke* was sometimes used as the past tense of *strike*, and *quoke* as the past tense of *quake*. In Early Modern English roosters usually *crew* rather than *crowed*, and boys often *slode* on the ice. And *sit* and *set*, *lie* and *lay* were used as unpredictably in Early Modern English as in the speech of some people today.

The verb *eat* is especially interesting. The past tense in Early Modern English was *at* or *ate* or especially *eat*, pronounced "et." In modern American English we always say "ate," but the British even today say "I 'et' my fish 'n' chips."

"He don't" and "It don't" were common in Early Modern English; in fact, the form *doesn't* has not been found in print before 1818. The contraction *an't* for *am not*, which developed into *ain't*, apparently originated in the late seventeenth century.

Other contractions, which now seem old-fashioned, include *'tis* for *it is (it's)*, *'twill* for *it will (it'll)*, and *'twas* for *it was*, for which we now have no short form. (Perhaps we should try to revive *'twas*.) Shakespeare's printer often spelled *I'll* as *Ile*.

The noun plural with *n*, which for a while had battled with *s*, almost vanished in Early Modern English. It still remains in *children, oxen, men*, and *women*, and in the rather rare words *kine* and *brethren*. Early Modern English sometimes used *eyen* for *eyes*, *shoon* for *shoes*, *hosen* for *hose*, and *peasen* for *peas*, as well as a number of others, but these disappeared from most dialects before 1700.

Possessives like "the king his crown" were fairly frequent in Early Modern English. Even "my moder ys sake" (my mother *his* sake) has been found, as well as "my sister her beauty." Apparently the reason for *his* in such constructions was that "the kinges crown" or "the kingys crown" sounded like "the king his crown." The apostrophe was seldom used to show possession until the late seventeenth century.

The London dialect during the E Mod E period became the standard one for the written or printed word, as it had started to do in Middle English. (Scottish people, though, long clung to their own preferences.) The spoken language, however, still had many dialects. A man named Richard Verstegnan wrote about the "different pronountiation" in the "severall parts" of England. A Londoner, he noted, would say "I would eat more cheese if I had it," but a Northerner would say "Ay sud eat mare cheese gin ay hadet," and a Westerner would say "Chud eat more cheese an chad it."

Punctuation and spelling are not technically parts of grammar, but a few comments on them may be included. In the earliest writing, for example in ancient Greek, there were no punctuation marks, although later Greeks used marks corresponding to our period, comma, and colon. OE manuscripts seldom used any punctuation except a centered period, but the ancestors of our question mark and hyphen were occasionally used in the tenth and eleventh centuries. ME manuscripts show little improvement, and the early printed books of Caxton also used punctuation sparingly and irregularly. (In this book most of the punctuation that you may have noticed in the OE and ME quotations was inserted by later editors.)

In Early Modern English a number of marks were used, first in Latin works and soon after in English ones. These marks were a period, a comma, a colon, a semicolon (with the comma *above* the period), a hyphen (two short parallel slanting lines), and an apostrophe to indicate the omission of a letter. There were no dashes, exclamation marks, parentheses, or brackets at this early time.

An Italian printer, Aldus Manutius (1450–1515), was largely responsible for the systematic development of punctuation. (He also invented italic type.) The rules he developed were intended to help the reader—still the only valid reason for using the marks. Although some changes and additions have been made since his day, we still follow his basic rules.

Early writing used no capital letters, but they gradually developed, especially in Middle English, from the large ornamental letters often drawn by scribes at the beginning of a new section. By Shakespeare's time capitals were pretty consistently used at the beginnings of sentences and for the names of people and places, though as late as 1484 William Caxton had printed Chaucer's name as *Gefferey chaucer.* Shakespeare's printers often capitalized important nouns even when they were not at the beginnings of sentences:

> The Play's the thing,
> Wherein Ile catch the Conscience of the King.
> (*Hamlet,* II, ii, 633–634)

But capital letters also show up in unpredictable spots. A system as nearly uniform as our own was not completely worked out for another couple of centuries.

Spelling in Early Modern English slowly became standardized, largely because printers thought there should be a correct way to spell every word. Previously, as we have seen, a scribe could spell a word almost any way he pleased—plesed—pleazed—pleezid. There were no dictionaries to show what was "right." By 1600, although many variations still existed, spelling was much less chaotic.

► In these few pages it has been possible to describe only a few of the major characteristics of Early Modern English. Your class may enjoy a careful scrutiny of one act, or even a single long scene, of a Shakespeare play, in order to study its grammar, punctuation, and spelling. Ideally, you should have a reprint of an early edition, since later editions usually include changes in the original printed spellings, in the punctuation marks, and, though more rarely, in the wording itself. But even if no early edition is available, you will be able to examine the verbs, adjectives, and other parts of speech, as well as the structure of the sentences. Doing so will make other plays by Shakespeare and other writings by his contemporaries much easier for you to read and to understand on the stage or on television.

6

the
language
from
1700
to the
present

1. Some Examples
of Eighteenth-Century English

SINCE you have probably read much in the literature of the nineteenth and twentieth centuries, it would be pointless to include examples here. But a few specimens of eighteenth-century writing may be worth a quick linguistic glance.

The first example is really late seventeenth century. It is part of Daniel Defoe's essay "The Education of Women" (1698). In this essay Defoe, best known for his *Robinson Crusoe*, showed that he was far ahead of his time by arguing that women deserved to be taught something more than housekeeping, embroidering, dancing, and the like. As you read this selection, note any small ways in which Defoe's language differs from that of today.

A woman well bred and well taught, furnished with the additional accomplishments of knowledge and behaviour, is a creature without comparison; her society is the emblem of sublimer enjoyments; her person is angelick and her conversation heavenly; she is all softness and sweetness, peace, love, wit, and delight. She is every way suitable to the sublimest wish, and the man that has such a one to his portion has nothing to do but to rejoice in her and be thankful.

On the other hand, suppose her to be the very same woman, and rob her of the benefit of education, and it follows thus:—

If her temper be good, want of education makes her soft and easy. Her wit, for want of teaching, makes her impertinent and talkative. Her knowledge, for want of judgement and experience, makes her fanciful and whimsical. If her temper be bad, want of breeding makes her worse, and she grows haughty, insolent, and loud. If she be passionate, want of manners makes her a termagant and a scold, which is much at one with lunatic. If she be proud, want of discretion (which still is breeding) makes her conceited, fantastic, and ridiculous. And from these she degenerates to be turbulent, clamorous, noisy, nasty, and the devil.

▶ What meaning does Defoe apparently use for *well bred, furnished, society, emblem, person, want, wit, passionate?* Which of these meanings are uncommon today?

▶ The word *termagant* is seldom used today. What is its meaning?

▶ What do *to his portion* (line 9) and *at one* (line 22) mean?

▶ Comment on the use of *be* in the third paragraph.

In 1716 John Gay published his long poem *Trivia: Or, The Art of Walking the Streets of London.* The following lines, describing the work of pickpockets, also show a number of other features of London life.

> Where the mob gathers, swiftly shoot along,
> Nor idly mingle in the noisy throng.
> *Lur'd* by the silver *hilt,* amid the swarm,
> The subtle *artist* will thy *side* disarm.
> Nor is thy *flaxen* wig with safety worn;
> High on the shoulder, in a basket borne,
> Lurks the sly boy; whose hand to *rapine* bred,
> Plucks off the *curling honours* of thy head.
> Here dives the skulking thief, with *practis'd sleight,*
> And unfelt fingers make thy pocket light.

Where's now thy watch, with all its *trinkets,*
    flown?
And thy *late* snuff-box is no more *thy* own.
But lo! his bolder thefts some *tradesman* spies,
Swift from his prey the *scudding lurcher* flies;
Dextrous he 'scapes the *coach* with nimble
    bounds,
Whilst ev'ry honest tongue "Stop thief" resounds.
So speeds the wily fox, alarm'd by fear,
Who lately *filch'd* the turkey's *callow care;*
Hounds *foll'wing* hounds grow louder as he flies,
And *injur'd* tenants join the hunter's cries.
Breathless he stumbling falls: ill-fated boy!
Why did not honest work thy youth employ?
Seiz'd by rough hands, he's dragg'd amid the *rout,*
And stretch'd beneath the pump's incessant
    spout:
Or plung'd in miry ponds, he gasping lies,
Mud chokes his mouth, and plasters *o'er* his eyes.

▶ Try to define or make some linguistic comment on each italicized word in the *Trivia* passage.

▶ Comment on the word order in any sentences that would be arranged differently today. To some extent the differences may be due to poetic license, but it is also true that eighteenth-century sentences did not follow set patterns quite as closely as sentences usually do now.

The next quotation is from Dr. Samuel Johnson, a big, blustery, and very learned man. He wrote many essays and biographies, and almost by himself compiled the first great dictionary of the English language. Much of his writing is marked (or marred) by long Latin-based words; as a result, his style has been called "sesquipedalian," a word that means "a foot and a half long." One of his most-quoted dictionary definitions, though not actually typical, is that for *network:* "anything reticulated or decussated at equal distances with interstices between the intersections."

This selection is from a somewhat less Latinized essay written by Johnson in 1759 for a magazine called *The Idler.* The words traceable to Latin are italicized.

Mr. Minim had now *advanced* himself to the *zenith* of *critical reputation;* when he was in the *pit,* every eye in the *boxes* was *fixed* upon him; when he *entered* his coffee-house, he was *surrounded* by *circles* of *candidates,* who *passed* their *novitiate* of *literature* under his *tuition;* his *opinion* was asked by all who had no *opinion* of their own, and yet loved to *debate* and *decide;* and no *composition* was *supposed* to *pass* in *safety* to *posterity,* till it had been *secured* by *Minim's approbation.*

Minim professes great *admiration* of the wisdom and *munificence* by which the *academies* of the *continent* were raised; and often wishes for some standard of *taste,* for some *tribunal,* to which *merit* may *appeal* from caprice, *prejudice,* and *malignity.* He has *formed* a *plan* for an *academy* of *criticism,* where every work of *imagination* may be read before it is *printed,* and which shall *authoritatively direct* the *theatres* what *pieces* to *receive* or *reject,* to *exclude* or to *revive.*

▶ Of the 166 words in that passage, what proportion are of Latin descent? How does this compare with what you noted on page 119?

▶ There are 116 different words in the passage. On that basis, what proportion of the words are Latin?

▶ Try to determine the meaning in Johnson's day for each of these words: *pit, boxes, candidates, novitiate, tuition, secured, academy, receive.* Paraphrase the passage (restate it in your own words), keeping the eighteenth-century meanings in mind.

▶ How long is Johnson's longest sentence? What is the average length of the three sentences?

▶ What do you think of Mr. Minim's idea of having an "academy" decide whether a book or a play is to be printed or performed? Do you know of any countries that have or once had such a regulation?

Now we'll look at some lines from Richard Brinsley Sheridan's comic play *The School for Scandal* (1777). Sir Peter Teazle is alone, thinking aloud.

SIR PETER T. When an old bachelor marries a young wife, what is he to expect? 'Tis now six months since Lady Teazle made me the happiest of men; and I have been the most miserable dog ever since! We tifted a little going to church, and fairly quarreled before the bells had done ringing. I was more than once nearly choked with gall during the honeymoon, and had lost all comfort in life before my friends had done wishing me joy. Yet I chose with caution—a girl bred wholly in the country, who never knew luxury beyond one silk gown, nor dissipation above the annual gala of a race ball [*a dance held after a day of horse racing*]. Yet she now plays her part in all the extravagant fopperies of fashion and the town, with as ready a grace as if she never had seen a bush or a grass-plot out of Grosvenor Square [*a small park in a fashionable district of London*]! I am sneered at by all my acquaintance, and paragraphed in the newspapers. She dissipates my fortune, and contradicts all my humours; yet the worst of it is, I doubt I love her, or I should never bear all this. However, I'll never be weak enough to own it.

► This Sheridan passage is obviously less formal than the ones by Defoe and Johnson. What evidence shows the informality?

► Sir Peter uses some words with slightly different meanings from the ones that are common today. Other words, though still used today, are rather rare. What do you suppose he means by *tifted, fairly, had done ringing, gall, dissipation, gala, extravagant, fopperies, ready, grace, paragraphed, contradicts, humours, doubt, own?* (A large dictionary may provide some clues.) Rewrite Sir Peter's speech in today's English, making sure that everything in it would be clear to anyone who went to see a modernized version of Sheridan's play.

Finally, let's look at some examples of eighteenth-century underworld slang collected by Francis Grose in 1785. All or most of these meanings for the terms have disappeared from the language. (As you know, slang terms generally have a short life, although some few of them survive and become standard.)

> *Babes in the woods.* Criminals in the stocks or pillory.
> *Barrel fever.* He died of the barrel fever: he killed himself by drinking.
> *Beau trap.* A loose stone in a pavement, under which water lodges, and, on being trod upon, squirts up.
> *Blubber cheeks.* Large, flaccid cheeks.
> *Bookkeeper.* One who never returns borrowed books.
> *Collar day.* Execution day.
> *Hen-house.* A house where the woman rules.
> *Peery.* Inquisitive, suspicious.

Scapegallows. One who deserves and has narrowly escaped the gallows.

Sea crab. A sailor.

Traps. Constables and thief-takers.

▶ Often slang is witty and descriptive. Which of the terms defined by Grose seem so to you? Why do you suppose they died out?

2. Developments in Pronunciation

On pages 124 to 125 we noted the Great Vowel Shift and some other changes in pronunciation that occurred between roughly 1500 and 1700. Some of these changes were not actually completed until the eighteenth century or later, and in some dialects never were completed. In some parts of England even today one may hear "stawn" for *stone*, "nahm" for *name*, "grayt" for *greet*, "cheeld" for *child*, "moan" for *moon*, "rum" for *room*, "farder" for *farther*, etc. (For some delightful tales illustrating the Yorkshire dialect, you might like to look up the short stories of Eric Knight, dealing with the adventures of Sam Snell, "the Flying Yorkshireman.")

No very big changes have occurred in the pronunciation of standard British English since 1700, though many small ones can be mentioned. The British call standard English "Received Standard," by which they mean the pronunciation and usage of the most highly educated Britishers. Received Standard is what one hears most of the time on BBC (the British Broadcasting Corporation network), and its use is encouraged at some of the most highly regarded secondary schools and universities. However, many of today's British schools seem to take the attitude that the Received Standard pronunciation really isn't very important, that there's nothing wrong with it for those who grew up with it but that there's nothing wrong with anybody else's variety either, if people can just understand what he says. This attitude is also appearing in many American schools, whose teachers once insisted that there is only one permissible pronunciation for each word.

Among the small changes in British pronunciation during the past couple of centuries has been the loss or reduction of the strong *r* sound in the middle or at the end of words. Today an Englishman is likely to say "pahk the cah," whereas if Shakespeare had owned an automobile, he would probably have said "pærk the cær," with both *r* sounds distinctly pronounced and with the /æ/ sound of *at* instead of the "ah" sound of *father*. Most Americans have retained the *r* sound, though "pahk the cah" may be heard in some sections of the East.

The /æ/ sound before *r* shifted to "ah," as the preceding example indicates. But the same thing happened in other circumstances too, with the "ah" sound now appearing in British pronunciations of such words as *craft, dance, branch, demand, can't, task, grasp, grass, last,* and *path*—maybe 150 to 200 words in all. It is not true, as many Americans seem to believe, that the British always use "ah" where we use /æ/. *Stamp, plastic,* and *gas,* for example, are pronounced with the /æ/ sound by most British speakers. Nevertheless, in a fair number of rather common words ("rah-thuh" is one of them), an "ah" sound did develop. One of the best examples is the word *what*, in which today both English and Americans use the "ah" sound but which Shakespeare apparently pronounced /wæt/ or /hwæt/. Similarly, in his day *was* seems to have been /wæs/.

A number of words that now have the long-*i* sound in *my* (really a diphthong) shifted to this sound after Early Modern English. Shakespeare and his contemporaries seem to have said "moy" for *my*, "thoy" for *thy*, "foyn" for *fine*, "oy" for *I*, etc. This pronunciation still survives in some British dialects, and in the nineteenth century was one of the marks of the stage Irishman.

In words ending in *-ery* or *-ary*, Americans retain the sound of the *e* or the *a*, but the British have largely lost it. So they say "cemet'ry," "mission'ry," "secret'ry," etc., while we say "cemetery," "missionary," "secretary," slightly accenting the *e* or the *a*. In effect, the British have chopped a syllable out of such words.

The rhymes used by poets offer some clues to pronunciation. In the early eighteenth century, for instance, Alexander Pope wrote:

Here thou, great Anna! whom three realms obey,
Dost sometimes counsel take—and sometimes
tea.

The rhyming of *obey* and *tea* suggests that in Pope's time *tea* was pronounced "tay." Pope also rhymed *glass* and *place*, *line* and *join*, *repair* and *ear*, *lost* and *boast*, and *grow* and *brow*.

Pronunciations continue to change even today. Your great-grandparents probably said "deef" for *deaf* and "jen-you-wine" for *genuine*. For many words today there are two or more pronunciations in standard English, and it is still uncertain which will win or whether both will continue. Examples are *advertisement, arctic, February, leisure,* and *almond.* The word *hegemony,* meaning "domination or leadership of one country in a group," has a total of at least six pronunciations listed in various modern dictionaries.

► How many common words can you think of that have variant pronunciations? Can you think of other words whose modern pronunciation differs from that of your great-grandparents?

Changes have occurred since Early Modern English not only in sounds but also in the placement of accent or stress. *Envy* used to be "en-VY," *welcome* was "wel-KUM," *character* was "kuh-RAK-ter," *antique* was "AN-teek," and *secure* was "SEE-kyure." In words like *concentrate* and *contemplate* the stress used to be on the second syllable; Americans and some British speakers now emphasize the first.

Sentence rhythms and intonation patterns of the past are difficult to determine, since we have no phonograph recordings from earlier periods. In all likelihood the patterns were somewhat different from those of today, but we cannot say just what the differences were. They may have been comparable to differences in modern British and American patterns, which are illustrated as follows by Thomas Pyles.[1] (The lines indicate high or low pitch.)

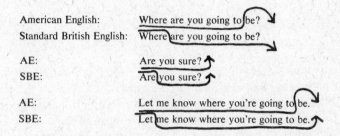

American English:	Where are you going to be?
Standard British English:	Where are you going to be?
AE:	Are you sure?
SBE:	Are you sure?
AE:	Let me know where you're going to be.
SBE:	Let me know where you're going to be.

Because of such differences in pitch patterns, Pyles says, an American in England who did no more than ask for a pack of cigarettes "would be spotted as a 'Yank' by practically any tobacconist in the British Isles." Similarly, if we could hear the pitch patterns of an earlier century, we would no doubt soon be able to identify the speaker as belonging to the seventeenth century or some other period.

▶ Your class may want to discuss some differences in pronunciation that you have noticed. For example, do members of your class pronounce certain words in different ways? Do people with varying foreign backgrounds use different pronunciations of English

---

[1] Pyles, *op. cit.*, p. 246.

words? Can you explain the differences? (In this discussion, remember that although a certain pronunciation may not happen to be standard now, it may have been standard in the past or may become so in the future.)

3. Vocabulary Changes

During the past two hundred years, the English language has continued to increase its vocabulary at a faster rate than ever, with new words or new meanings developing not only in England but also in the United States, Canada, and other English-speaking countries. The 1973 *World Book Dictionary*, for instance, listed a hundred or so recently created words and words used with new meanings. Among them:

eye•wall (ī′wôl′), *n.* a layer of turbulent clouds around the eye, or calm center, of a storm: *Planes flew there to dump their crystals, in hopes of causing supercooled water droplets in the hurricane's eyewall to condense* (Science News).

in•ca•pac•i•tant (in′kə pas′ə tənt), *n.* a chemical agent or drug that temporarily induces sleepiness, dizziness, disorientation, etc.: *One of the standard US incapacitants produces dizziness, heart palpitation, urinary retention and constipation* (New Scientist).

re•jas•ing (rē jā′sing), *n. U.S. Slang.* the act or practice of putting rubbish or discarded items to useful purpose: *The biggest benefit of*

*rejasing is that virtually indestructible objects
never reach the garbage heap* (Time). [*reusing
junk as something else*]

urb (ėrb), *n.* a large urban area; megalopolis:
*The growth of American suburbia, fed by the
yearning for a home of one's own, raises
problems for urb and suburb alike* (New York
Times). [shortened for *urban*]

It is impossible to say how many words there are in
the English language, because even the largest dictionary does not contain all of them; besides, today's
total would be different tomorrow. Languages of
other countries have also grown very rapidly during
the past couple of centuries, but the total increase
in English vocabulary is probably greatest because
of the wide spread of English around the world.
English could be expected to grow faster than French,
for example, because it has a larger number of
speakers. And although more people speak Chinese
than English, the Chinese vocabulary is at present
not nearly so large as that of English, perhaps because most of the Chinese live in only one part of the
world.

As was true in the past, English in recent times has
borrowed many words from other languages. The
rate of borrowing from Latin, however, declined
after 1675, but nevertheless Latin has contributed
thousands of words since that time. Of the twenty
thousand most-used words in the English language
today, about twelve thousand are derived from Latin.
Another four thousand are modern forms of OE
words, and the rest are from other languages.

French has continued to contribute. Examples from
the past three centuries include the cooking terms

casserole, marinade, braise, and *sauté;* hungry people even in earlier years were indebted to the French for *omelet, sauce, biscuit,* and *dessert.* Today *hors d'oeuvres* are served at countless parties, thousands of restaurants serve *filet mignon,* and many menus disguise beans as *haricots* or peas as *petits-pois;* some persons who would be horrified at the thought of eating a snail or a crayfish look upon an *escargot* or an *écrevisse* as a great delicacy. Some of these words, like *haricot* and *escargot,* are beginning to find their way into English dictionaries; others haven't yet made the grade. It is interesting to speculate about the exact stage at which any borrowed word becomes "English."

Borrowings from other languages are widely scattered. Here are just a few examples from the many since 1700:

anaconda (Singhalese)	gumbo (African)
attar (Persian)	hibachi (Japanese)
babushka (Russian)	juke (African)
bandanna (Hindustani)	karate (Japanese)
bangle (Hindustani)	kismet (Turkish)
basenji (Afrikaans)	kiwi (Maori)
beriberi (Singhalese)	kosher (Yiddish)
caddy (Malay)	kumquat (Chinese)
caftan (Turkish)	luau (Hawaiian)
calaboose (Spanish)	machismo (Spanish)
carom (Spanish)	mazurka (Polish)
dachshund (German)	mustang (Spanish)
drawl (Dutch)	nickel (Swedish)
flak (German)	paprika (Hungarian)
ghoul (Arabic)	picaresque (Spanish)
goulash (Hungarian)	Podunk (Algonquian)
graffiti (Italian)	pogrom (Russian)

polka (Czech)	temblor (Spanish)
raffia (Malagasy)	trattoria (Italian)
robot (Czech)	trek (Afrikaans)
safari (Swahili)	ukase (Russian)
sauerbraten (German)	ukulele (Hawaiian)
sauna (Finnish)	vamoose (Spanish)
shampoo (Hindi)	wallaby (Australian)
sukiyaki (Japanese)	yak (Tibetan)

The British have on occasion adopted American words, despite the fact that they have often expressed contempt for these "Americanisms" from across the Atlantic. Thomas Jefferson's *belittle*, at first vigorously attacked by the British, is now not infrequent. *Blizzard* and *cloudburst* are weather terms that they have borrowed; *prairie* and *swamp* are geographical terms; *bunk* (or *bunkum* or *buncombe*) and *caucus* are political in origin. American *radio* and British *wireless* are both used; so are American *TV* and British *telly* as convenient shortenings for *television*. *Movies* is as familiar a word in England as *cinema*. Other rather recent borrowings from America include *highbrow* and *lowbrow*, *filling station*, *star* (in the movies), *show business*, *stooge*, and *sales-resistance*. The American *two weeks* is threatening to oust the traditional British *fortnight*.

But borrowing words from other countries is just one of the ways in which the vocabulary of a language grows. Though English has always been a quite enthusiastic borrower, it has also greatly increased its word-stock by forming new words in a number of different ways. We'll look at a variety of examples of these neologisms (a fancy name for "new words"), some fairly recent, others dating back several centuries.

Compounding. Compounding is an old method that is still used. Someone sees, for instance, berries that are black, so he calls them *blackberries*. A man invents a game that requires players to hit a ball and run around bases; he calls it *baseball*. A boxer knocks another boxer unconscious, and sportswriters write about the *knockout*. (*Sportswriter* is itself another compound.) Some compounds change form and no longer look like a combination of two words: *barn*, for instance, resulted in Anglo-Saxon times from the compounding of *bere* (barley) and *ærn* (place). The Anglo-Saxon words for *lord* and *lady* were both compounds. In Old English *lord* was *hlāfweard*; *hlāf* meant "loaf (of bread)," and *weard* was "guardian"; literally, a lord was the "guardian of the bread." *Hlāfweard* went through a series of sound changes (*hlaford, laford, laword*, for example) and finally came out *lord*. The lord's wife was a *hlāfdīge*, the "kneader of the bread."

Some compounds are originally written as two words, later with a hyphen, and still later as a solid word. In the past century the name of a popular sport has changed from *basket ball* to *basket-ball* to the present *basketball*. A compound term written as separate words is called an "open" compound. Many of our compounds remain open: *ice cream, bird dog, fire engine, master of ceremonies*, etc.

► Try to think of other compound words like the ones[2] at the top of the following page.

---

[2]The classifications given are based on Bryant, *op. cit.*, p. 242.

verb plus noun: *whirlwind*
verb plus adverb: *touchdown*
adverb plus verb: *input*
noun plus adjective: *watertight*
phrase oddities: *hand-to-mouth*

Combining with affixes.   Another way to create new words is to attach an affix—a prefix or a suffix—to an existing word. Say that we start with the noun *grace*. We add *-ful* to it and have the adjective *graceful*, and by adding *-ly* to that we get the adverb *gracefully*. We can also add to the other end, getting *ungraceful* and *ungracefully*, *disgrace*, *disgraceful*, *disgracefully*.

Some prefixes and suffixes, such as *un-*, *re-*, *-ness*, and *-able*, become parts of thousands of new words. *Un-*, for example, can be placed before scores of adjectives: *unkind*, *unreal*, *unpopular*, *unsafe*, etc., or, with a different meaning, before many verbs: *undo*, *unfasten*, *unwind*, *uncover*, etc. *Re-* is freely prefixed to verbs: *reassert*, *refold*, *retell*, *recapture*. The suffix *-able* can be attached to dozens of verbs and nouns, as in *singable*, *readable*, *breakable*, *enjoyable*, *washable*, *comfortable*, *peaceable*. And the suffix *-ness* converts countless adjectives into nouns: *bigness*, *kindness*, *flakiness*, *carelessness*, *preparedness*, and so on.

Though most affixes remain in use for centuries, some of them gradually die out. Once, for instance, *-dom* and *-hood* were common suffixes, showing up in such words as *kingdom*, *wisdom*, *manhood*, and *likelihood*, but today they are rarely used in making new words. The prefix *ante-* is also uncommon in word formation today, having been largely replaced by *pre-*.

▶ Make a list of several commonly used prefixes and suffixes, other than those named above, and write four or five words in which each one appears.

▶ The class is to take a few common words like *accept, compete, compose, critic, defend, effect, globe, heart, legal, magnet, predict, sane,* and *visit,* and think of other words that can be made from each by the addition of affixes. (Sometimes a slight change in spelling is involved, as in *defensible* from *defend*.)

▶ What is the root word and what are the affixes in *antidisestablishmentarianism?*

Back-formations. Much less important, but rather interesting, is a process called "back-formation." Here, instead of adding, something is taken off an old word to make a new one. From the adjective *enthusiastic,* for instance, has come the verb *enthuse,* which some people are not willing to accept as "good

English." Yet these same people use *edit* (formed in the same way from *editor*), *jell* (from *jelly*), *peeve* (from *peevish*), and *reminisce* (from *reminiscence*), though this last one has gained respectability only rather recently.

▶ Which words would you guess the following back-formations came from—*peddle, buttle, burgle, orate, greed, diagnose, emote, resurrect?* Check your guesses in a dictionary.

Onomatopoeia. Some words are created to imitate sounds, by a process sometimes called "onomatopoeia" or "echoism." Whoever long ago named the bird *cuckoo* simply coined a name that sounds like— or suggests—the call of the bird. Other examples are *fizz, gurgle, twitter, swish,* and *bow-wow.* Interestingly enough, though, different languages do not choose the same imitative sounds: Spanish dogs say *guau,* French dogs say *gnaf-gnaf,* Yugoslavian dogs say *av-av,* German ones say *wau-wau,* and Japanese ones say *wung-wung.*

▶ What other imitative words can you think of? Try to coin one or two of your own to name sounds or objects that make sounds in your household or school.

Clipped forms. Sometimes a word is shortened—or "clipped"—without a different part of speech resulting, as is the case in back-formation. *Mob* used to be *mobile vulgus*, a term seldom used since the seventeenth century. *Fan* (such as a baseball fan) was clipped from *fanatic;* both words are still in the language, though their meanings are now seldom identical. *Prof* is an informal shortening of *professor, bus* of *omnibus, plane* of *airplane*. The clipping may be done from the beginning or from the end of a word, as these examples show.

► What are the older, long forms of *gym, auto, copter, zoo, prop, mike, tarp, fridge, photo, trig, phone?*

► With the aid of a dictionary, find the words from which *spite, sport, still* (for making whiskey), *lone,* and *fence* came. Can you think of any other clipped forms—both old and new?

Blends. A different kind of shortening, called "blending," involves "telescoping" two words to form a new word neatly combining the meaning of the two. *Brunch,* a combination of *breakfast* and *lunch,* and *motel (motor + hotel)* are perhaps the best-known examples. Lewis Carroll blended *chuckle* and *snort* to form *chortle*, and coined *galumph* from a blend of *gallop* and *triumph*. Walter Winchell telescoped *infant* and *anticipate*, coining *infanticipate* to use in his gossip column; other rather amusing blends like *cinemactress (cinema + actress), alcoholiday (alcohol + holiday), glamazon (glamor + amazon), anecdotage (anecdote + dotage)*, and *insinuendo (insinuate + innuendo)* may be found in today's newspaper and magazine writing.

▶ What words do you suppose are blended in *smog, cinemaddict, boatel, slanguage, sneet* (a form of precipitation), *electrocute, camporee?* (An unabridged dictionary may help you with some of these if you are baffled.)

Words from names. The names of people or places are still another source of new words. *Derrick* was the name of a hangman in London around 1600; in time his name came to be used for the gallows, and later for today's device for lifting, which looks a little like a gallows. Electrical terms derived from names of men include *ohm, watt, volt,* and *ampere*. The British policeman is called *bobby* because Sir *Robert* Peel once reorganized the London police system; smug conformity to middle-class ideals is called *babbittry* because this conformity was the outstanding trait of George F. Babbitt, the main character in Sinclair

Lewis's novel *Babbitt*. And the names of places that are in some way closely associated with various products have frequently been the source of names for those products: *bourbon* (from *Bourbon* County, Kentucky), *cologne* (from *Cologne*, Germany), *millinery* (from *Milan*, Italy), *mayonnaise* (from *Mahón*, Minorca), *oxford* (from *Oxford*, England), and *dumdum* (from *Dum Dum*, an arsenal near Calcutta, India), to name only a few.

▶ Turn to your dictionary to find the proper nouns that were the source of *mesmerize, sandwich, silhouette, boycott, timothy, casaba, stogie, badminton, boysenberry, jeans, wisteria.*

True coinages. Very few words are coined without reliance on some earlier word or words. Perhaps the best example is *Kodak,* a group of letters that George Eastman thought interesting. In the early 1970's a computer aided in the search for a catchy new name for an old brand of gasoline: *Exxon* was the result. *Spoof,* coined by Arthur Roberts, a British comedian, and *blurb* and *goop,* coined by Gelett Burgess, also belong in this small group of true creations.

Acronyms. Acronyms are words formed from the initial letters or syllables of other words. In World War II various women's military groups were known as *Wacs* (from *W*omen's *A*rmy *C*orps), *Waves*

(*W*omen *A*ccepted for *V*olunteer *E*mergency *S*ervice), *Spars* (from *S*emper *Par*atus, the motto of the Coast Guard), and *Wrens* (*W*omen's *R*oyal *N*aval *S*ervice). Trained military dogs were called the *K-9* Corps, an unusual acronym in which *K* represents *Ca-* and *9* represents *-nine*. Americans have been asked to send contributions to CARE—*C*ooperative for *A*merican *R*emittances to *E*verywhere, Inc. In World War I the British *D*efence *o*f the *R*ealm *A*ct became known as *Dora*. *Radar* comes from "*ra*dio *d*etecting *a*nd *r*anging," and NASA is the *N*ational *A*eronautics and *S*pace *A*dministration. Sometimes a person in military service is AWOL (*a*bsent *w*ithout *l*eave). A *w*hite *A*nglo-*S*axon *P*rotestant may be called a WASP for short. A true acronym is not just a group of initials, but a group pronounceable as a word—as these examples show.

► Make a list of as many acronyms as you can recall.

Functional shift. Sometimes a word that starts out as one part of speech is shifted to function as another. In such "functional shift," the shifted word takes on the characteristics of the other part of speech—in one sense, it *becomes* the other part of speech. A noun converted to serve as a verb, for instance, will take on verb endings and will team with auxiliaries like *will, has, are, were,* etc. Let's use a nonsense word to see how this works. Let's suppose you have

165

in your vocabulary the word *glag*. *Glag* is a noun, since you use it in sentences like this: "I have plenty of glag"; "The glag is on the table"; "Ed bought two glags today." Now even though *glag* is a noun, you are free to make it do the work of a verb, simply by treating it as a verb. So you can say such things as "She glagged the room" or "I will glag her room tomorrow." And there is nothing to stop you from talking about a "glag doll" or a "narrow glag strip," making *glag* a modifier. If you substitute *paper* for *glag*, you'll see how this sort of thing happened with a real word.

► Many thousands of English words can be used as more than one part of speech. With the aid of a dictionary, if necessary, make up sentences in which you use the following:

1. *out* as adverb, adjective, preposition, noun, verb
2. *down* as adverb, adjective, preposition, noun, verb
3. *like* as adjective, noun, preposition, conjunction, adverb

One of the problems in counting the words in a person's vocabulary or in a language is that many words have more than a single meaning. If, for instance, a person knows two meanings for *chair* (a *chair* to sit on; to *chair* a meeting), should *chair* be counted as two words or one? The *Thorndike-Barnhart Advanced Dictionary* lists for *light* in its various senses (not dark; not heavy; come to ground, etc.) a total of 49 definitions, not including its use in phrases like *shed light on* and *light in the head.* For *run* it lists 78 definitions besides those for its use in phrases like *run down* and *in the long run.* If we were to try to count the total words in the English language, should we count *light* and *run* only once each, or as a combined total of 127, or as some other total obtained by checking in a different dictionary? One scholar, in fact, thought that he could detect 829 different meanings for *run.* If we accepted his figure for this, and similar figures for other words with multiple meanings, the total English vocabulary would reach into the millions.

It should be remembered that place-names and names of people are words too. Our individual vocabularies, as well as the total vocabulary, contain many words of these kinds.

Place-names, in England and elsewhere, are derived in various ways. Some are so old that their original meanings are lost. Some are borrowed: names with *-chester* or *-cester,* such as *Manchester* and *Leicester,* are based on Latin *castra* (camp). *Charing Cross,* the name of a district in London, is borrowed from Norman-French; it was at a square here that Edward I put a cross in honor of Eleanor of Castille, his *"chère reine"* (dear queen). And some names are descriptive: *Oxford* is so named because centuries ago the river there had a ford where oxen could cross. Mario Pei gives this amusing account of one such name:

Near Plymouth rises a ridge called Torpenhow Hill. *Tor* is Saxon for "hill"; *pen* is the Celtic word for "head" or "hill," added later, when the force of *Tor* was lost; *how* is the Scandinavian *haugr*, which also means "hill" or "height." Last came Middle English speakers on whom the force of the earlier words was spent. Their final contribution makes the name Hillhillhill Hill![3]

People's last names come mainly from fathers' names, places, personal characteristics, and occupations. (Most people had only one name until a few centuries ago.) The numerous names ending in *son* or beginning with *Mac* or *Mc* mean "son of _____." Of these the most interesting is *Johnson*, because it appears in different spellings in many languages. *Johnson* is English for "son of John," *Jones* is Welsh, *Hanson* or *Hansen* or *Jansen* or *Jensen* or *Johannsen* is usually Scandinavian, *Ivanovich* is Russian with the same meaning, and the name appears in variant forms in several other languages. Some ancestor of every person with a name like *Manchester, York,* or *Glasgow* was pretty obviously named for a place. People called *Long, Short, Brown, Langbane* (long bone), or *Stout* no doubt had an ancestor who was described in that way, even though today's Mr. Short may be six feet six. Names based on occupations are represented by *Smith* and *Smythe, Miller* and *Mueller* (German), *Wagner* or *Waggoner, Taylor,* and *Cooper* (a maker of barrels).

▶ What persons' names can you think of for each of the four types?

[3]Mario Pei, *The Story of English*, Philadelphia: J. B. Lippincott Co. 1952, p. 127.

Many first names are taken from the Bible: *Adam, Joshua, Matthew, Mark, Luke,* and *John,* for instance. Some, like *Alexander* and *Julius,* are names of famous historical figures. *Alvin* and *Bernard* go back to old German words meaning "noble friend" and "bold as a bear." *Earl* and *Alfred* are among the survivors from Anglo-Saxon. *Ian* is a Gaelic form of *John. Homer* is Greek. *Algernon* is French. *Milton* and *Mitchell* were once just surnames. Perhaps the most religious first name on record is one mentioned by Dr. Pei: If-Christ-Had-Not-Died-For-Thee-Thou-Hadst-Been-Damned Barebone, shortened by his friends to *Damned Barebone.*

Girls' first names often come from the same sources. In addition, flower names have often been used: *Rose, Violet, Lily,* etc. At one time many girls were named for admired virtues: *Faith, Hope, Charity,* and even *Humility* and *Purity.* Some girls' names are feminine counterparts of masculine names: *Geraldine* from *Gerald, Jessie* from *Jess, Joan* from *John, Julia* from *Julius.* In general, though, if we trace girls' names back to their original meanings, we find that they usually denoted something beautiful, angelic, happy, or sweet, while boys' names generally denoted something bold, strong, warlike, noble, courageous, or the like.

▶ If a dictionary with a section devoted to given names is available, members of the class may enjoy looking up the derivations and original meanings of a number of their names.

Once a word gets into the language, it doesn't always stay the same. Besides changing in pronunciation and spelling, it may change in meaning and perhaps become more respectable or less so. The word *nice*, for instance, once meant "foolish" or "silly." Later it came to mean "foolishly picky or fastidious," a meaning that survives in *nicey-nice*. Still later it meant (and in some contexts still means) "precise" or "very accurate," as in "a *nice* distinction." And today, if we say "a *nice* day," the word simply means "pleasant," very different from the original "silly."

Silly itself goes back to Anglo-Saxon *sælig*, meaning "happy" or "good." At a later time it meant "helpless" or "frail" or "sickly," and then "rustic" or "humble." Next it meant "weak in intellect," and from this our present meaning developed.

In centuries past, men wore *bonnets*, but today, except perhaps in Scotland and a few other places, that privilege is reserved for ladies and babies. *Fond* once meant "foolish"; since a young man who is fond of a girl may still do and say some foolish things, maybe that meaning has changed less than it seems. A *charm* was once a "magic spell," as in the *Macbeth* witches' "Peace! The charm's wound up." A *smock* was formerly a "lady's undergarment." When you hear someone say, "The exception proves the rule," the chances are that he does not know that at the time when the expression was first used, *to prove* meant "to test"; therefore the intended meaning was that the exception *tests* the rule.

Among words that have gained in reputation are *knight*, which once used to mean simply a "boy"; *enthusiasm*, once almost a synonym for "madness"; *minister*, at one time a "servant"; *paradise*, from an

Old Persian word for park; and *Quaker*, once a term of ridicule but now used without any unfavorable overtones for a member of a highly regarded religious group.

Other words have followed the path of pejoration—downhill—rather than that of elevation. *Immoral* once meant "not customary," and once a *vice* was only a "minor flaw of character." *Hussy* was originally the same word as *housewife*, and *knave* was once any boy—rascal or not. (The German *Knabe*, which still means "boy," was once the same word.) In the beginning a *villain* was simply a farm laborer; a *counterfeiter* used to be anyone who copied or imitated anything, though today he is usually thought of as someone who copies with the intention of cheating.

Sometimes a word suffers only a temporary setback. A *collaborator* is a person who works with another. But during World War II the French people who more or less willingly worked with the German invaders were sneeringly called "collaborators," and so for a few years no one at all wanted that title. Now, however, this useful word has regained its respectability.

Words may become broader in meaning—or narrower. *Arrive*, in its original Latin form, meant "to the shore," but its meaning so broadened that one may arrive at school, in the city, on the moon, or anywhere else. The word *mill* once meant only "a place where grain is ground." (The word *meal*, as in *corn meal*, is from the same source.) Now a *mill* doesn't necessarily grind anything: we have steel mills, woolen mills, cotton mills, etc. Narrowing is illustrated by *meat*, which in the King James Bible (1611) meant "solid food of any type," but now means "animal flesh used as food." *Starve* once meant "to die" (in any way whatsoever) but was narrowed to mean "to die of hunger." Now it is often used to mean nothing more than "to feel very hungry."

Many words and meanings of words die. In the 1920's some styles of automobiles were called *touring cars* (open cars with folding tops, carrying four or more passengers), *runabouts* (open one-seated cars), or *coupés* (closed cars, usually with a single seat). One nineteenth-century closed carriage was called a *brougham* (named for Lord Brougham and pronounced "broom," or "broo-um" or "broh-um"). When vehicles of these particular types disappeared from the scene, their names did too.

A number of words used by Shakespeare and his contemporaries have since died. Usually such words first become "obsolescent," that is, dying or little used; later they become "obsolete"—dead. In the first act of *Macbeth,* for instance, we find among such words *alarum* (alarm, a trumpet call), *kerns* and *gallowglasses* (light-armed and heavy-armed troops), *nave* (naval), *memorize* (in the sense of *commemorate*), *aroint* (go away), and *posters* (rapid travelers).

► Look at a scene from *Macbeth* or another Shakespearean play to find out whether it contains any words now obsolete or at least obsolescent. Check a dictionary in doubtful cases.

4. Developments in Grammar

Today's sentences are somewhat more fixed in word order than were those of Shakespeare's time.

Although flexibility still exists, most modern sentences follow one of these patterns:

a. S–V (subject–verb):   Pelicans glide.
b. S–V–O (subject–verb–object):   Pelicans eat fish.
c. S–V–PN (subject–verb–predicate noun):
Pelicans are birds.
d. S–V–PA (subject–verb–predicate adjective):
Pelicans are large.

Over 90 percent of modern simple sentences (excluding questions and commands) follow one of these four patterns, with *b* the most common, followed by *a*, *c*, and *d*. The presence of modifiers does not affect the pattern. For example, if we say "The two fat pelicans ate the tiny fish greedily," the pattern is still *b*.

Questions and commands, as well as sentences of the type "There is a pelican in my bathtub," are variations of the basic four types.

In the English of Shakespeare's time, in contrast, the subject was quite often not the first main part of a sentence. Here are a few examples, from *Macbeth:*

> My noble partner
> You greet with present grace . . .   (I, iii, 48–49)

> As thick as hail
> Came post with post [messenger after messenger]
> . . .   (I, iii, 97–98)

> This have I thought good to deliver thee . . .   (I, v, 10–11)

Although the present patterns were well developed by the sixteenth and seventeenth centuries, authors took more liberties in word arrangement than most of them do now.

On pages 121–124 we commented on the increased use of *do* in questions and negatives since Shakespeare's time, and also pointed out a few other developments. We'll take a quick look now at several others.

In the seventeenth and eighteenth centuries, many authors tended to write a high proportion of long sentences. In an essay written in 1644 by John Milton, for instance, four consecutive sentences chosen at random run 85, 72, 50, and 52 words, an average of about 65. Sentences began to get somewhat shorter in the nineteenth century, though in some magazines the average was still about 40 words. Today's English sentences average only about 20 words.

▶ Be prepared to discuss this question in class: Are short sentences better than long?

Several things have happened to verbs. One is the steady and almost unnoticed growth of what are called "two-word verbs" or "verb-adverb combinations." We say "I *ran across* an odd bit of information." Actually, we didn't *run,* and we didn't go *across* anything. The two words together are in effect a new verb with the meaning "found" or "happened on" (another verb-adverb combination). Here are a few others, including some three-word ones, among more than a thousand now in the language. Their intended meaning, in context, is immediately clear.

> Another dancer *cut in*.
> The big boys *picked on* me.
> We *ran out of* money.
> He *went on* talking.
> They *held up* a bank.
> We *set out* for home.
> When I *came to*, it was dark.
> Sammy *is up to* some mischief.
> I have to *check with* my father.
> She *went back on* her word.
> I'll *make up for* my mistake.
> She *rang up* the sale.

▶ Make a list of additional examples of verb-adverb combinations. Use each in a short sentence. Why are such verbs likely to be confusing to a foreigner learning our language?

A battle has long gone on about the few "strong verbs" that have survived from Old English. You will recall that these are the irregular verbs, those that do not use *-d* or *-ed* in the past tense and past participle: e.g., *know, knew, (have) known* in contrast to the weak verb *call, called, (have) called*. In the eighteenth century, *(have) wrote* and *(have) written* fought it out, with *(have) written* finally winning, although the original title of a famous poem by Thomas Gray was

"Elegy Wrote in a Country Churchyard." *Knew* and *known* finally won out over *knowed*, though that form is still heard in some people's speech. *(Have) spoke* battled with *(have) spoken*, the issue being further complicated by still another form, *spake*. A number of other verbs went through similar struggles. The battle still hasn't completely ended for some verbs; past tense *sang* and *rang* still fight rear-guard actions against *sung* and *rung*.

Quite a few strong verbs have moved over to the more numerous weak faction, some of them in recent centuries. Among these are *dread, fare, flow, fold, gnaw, heave, help, knead, laugh, mourn, scrape, wade, wash*, and *weigh*. If this change had not occurred, none of these verbs would have the *-d* or *-ed* they now have in the past and past participle. In fact, instead of saying "I *laughed* at her" and "I have *laughed*," we might be saying "I *loog* at her" and "I have *laggen*."

The growth of verb phrases has been considerable. Many of these with infinitives (verbs with *to*) increased in popularity in the eighteenth century: *seemed to be, used to come*, etc. But much longer phrases are now used daily, and are very vexatious to foreigners, who get lost in the wilderness of *might have been expected to appear* or *will have been being advised to retreat*. Fortunately most of the verb phrases are less bewildering, and they do follow a definite pattern. For example, take

     may have been eating

For *may* it is possible to substitute *must* or one of the other modals *(can, could, might, will, shall, would, should)*, but *have, been*, and the *-ing* form never change, regardless of the main verb we are using. Or, in

   is being eaten

although *am*, *are*, *was*, or *were* may be used instead of *is*, the forms *being* and *eaten* (or whatever the past participle is) remain the same. Grammarians have made clear how basically simple the patterns of most verb phrases are. It is because of that simplicity that most native speakers master them by the age of ten or twelve.

▶ Make a list of verb phrases following each of these patterns:

   a. is eating (Use *are*, *was*, *were*, as well as *is;* use verbs besides *eat.*)
   b. is being eaten (same directions as for *a*)
   c. may be eating (Use *might*, *can*, *could*, *will*, *would*, *shall*, *should*, *must*, as well as *may;* use verbs besides *eat.*)
   d. may have been eating (same directions as for *c*)
   e. may have been eaten (same directions as for *c*)
   f. has eaten (Use *have*, *had*, as well as *has;* use verbs besides *eat.*)
   g. has been eaten (same directions as for *f*)

The use of the passive voice has increased in recent centuries. Although in Shakespeare's time one might say "The pigs were eaten by the wolf," the active form "The wolf ate the pigs" was more likely. Today we still favor the active but use the passive with considerable frequency. In the nineteenth century "The house is being built" (a progressive passive form, showing that the building was in progress) was considered bad English, and "The house is building" was favored. Today the latter sentence would rarely be heard.

A somewhat similar change can be observed in a sentence like "The athletes were awarded gold medals." Only a hundred or so years ago this sentence would have been attacked on the ground that it was the medals, not the athletes, that were awarded. American short-story writer Ambrose Bierce, for instance, wrote a book called *Write It Right* in which he said:

> *Given.* "The soldier was given a rifle." What was given is the rifle, not the soldier. "The house was given a coat (coating) of paint." Nothing can be "given" anything.

Today the sentences attacked by Bierce would, of course, be considered normal.

Before the eighteenth century comparatively few people seemed to worry much about "correctness" in language. Nobody wrote a book called *Write It Right*. But the eighteenth century was a period when many people believed in regularity and conformity. They thought that the English language should be as regular and free from variation as Latin was. They often forgot, however, that English was a living language and that Latin no longer had any native speakers;

even the Romans were speaking Italian, which like Spanish and Portuguese and French had been derived from Latin but was quite different.

The Italians and the French had created "academies" that were designed to control the language and prevent any "impurities" from entering. Even though these academies were not successful in this goal—because Italian and French were living, developing languages too—some Englishmen thought there should be an English academy for the same purpose. Jonathan Swift was one of the prime leaders of the movement, and perhaps a national academy would have been formed if Queen Anne had lived longer. But since George I, who became king in 1714, was of the German House of Hanover and had little interest in the English language, Swift lost his battle for an academy.

► Suppose that an academy had been formed to control the language. What do you suppose are some of the steps it might have taken? To what extent do you believe it could have been successful?

Even without an academy, though, efforts to regulate the language went on. Bishop Robert Lowth in 1762 published his *Short Introduction to English Grammar,* in which he criticized the "errors" of Chaucer, Shakespeare, and other earlier writers and explained what they should have written. An "error" to Lowth and his followers was anything that they themselves happened not to like. They didn't like, for

179

example, the split infinitive, as in "to seldom call," because they admired Latin, and in Latin it is impossible to split an infinitive; *vocare* (to call) is a single word and obviously can't be split. So English, they argued, should be like Latin and not chop up its infinitives the way that Shakespeare, Milton, and others had done. They paid no attention to the fact that English is Germanic, not Latin-based, in its grammar.

So Lowth and his followers, both in England and in America, began to compile rules by the hundreds to govern the use of English. Some of the rules were sensible enough. For example, it seems reasonable to use the plural *were* rather than the singular *was* after the plural pronoun *they: they were* rather than *they was*. And it probably makes sense to get rid of the unnecessary *at* in *Where is it at?* But the rulemakers also objected to *Where did you come from?* on the ground that in Latin a preposition like *from* must always come before its object, so they insisted on *From where did you come?*—a construction that sounds awkward and pedantic to modern ears.

But we shouldn't be too hard on Bishop Lowth and his followers. Many people in those days (and even today) were saying, in effect, "Somebody please help me with my English! I want to learn to speak and write properly. I need good English if I am to be successful in my work or in my social life. I hate it when someone raises an eyebrow because of the way I express myself. Somebody please tell me the rules I should follow." Bishop Lowth and the others were merely trying to give the public what the public was clamoring for. People bought Lowth's little book in great numbers—twenty-two editions were published.

Teachers of English generally welcomed the rules. Latin teachers could refer to unbreakable rules, they argued, so why shouldn't English teachers? But some of them went so far in their insistence on such unnatural expressions as *From where did you come?* that they made their students think that use of the language was hemmed in by thousands of silly restrictions. Some students worried so much about the restrictions that they lost whatever ability they might have had to write and speak imaginatively and without unnecessary tension.

Today's teachers usually try to find a middle road between complete freedom (which is anarchy) and complete adherence to all the rules that somebody dreamed up. They know, for example, that most employers like to have employees whose language will not be embarrassingly nonconforming; they usually want their employees to say, for instance, *We were* and *He and I went* rather than *We was* and *Me and him went*. But teachers also know that the rules about *whom* and *shall* are no longer rigid, if they ever were, and that it is ridiculous to insist on *From where did you come?*

▶ Suppose that you were a teacher of English faced with the problem of teaching rules of usage like those we have been considering. How much of such teaching would you try to do? Are there some expressions that you would strongly condemn? Would you try to make the point that usage changes and that some expressions used by educated people today were once "incorrect," and vice versa? Would you try to get across the concept of appropriateness—that the situation, the speaker, and the audience often determine whether a particular usage is appropriate or not? In general, what principles would you try to follow in teaching usage?

5. Dictionaries

The early dictionaries, dating back to the Middle Ages, were simply definitions in Latin of unusual Latin words. Later dictionaries gave translations of difficult Latin words into English or of English words into Latin. The first all-English dictionary did not appear until 1604, when Robert Cawdrey published "*A Table Alphabeticall of Hard Words*, conteyning and teaching the true writing and vnderstanding of hard vnvsuall English wordes, borrowed from the Hebrew, Greeke, Latine, or French, &c." The first book to use the word *dictionary* in the modern sense was Henry Cockeram's *English Dictionarie* (1623). Its subtitle was *Interpreter of Hard English Words*, and it promised "the more speedy Attaining of an Elegant Perfection of the English Tongue" by "Ladies and Gentlewomen, young Schollers, Clarkes, Merchantes, as also Strangers of any Nation."

Not until the eighteenth century did any dictionary try to include most or all English words, and not just the "hard ones." Most early dictionaries had listed only a few hundred or a few thousand words, but one published in 1706 had 38,000 and Nathan Bailey's *Dictionarium Britannicum* (1730) had 48,000. Bailey's *Universal Etymological English Dictionary* (1721) was one of the first that systematically tried to show the etymologies (derivations) of words; it was Bailey, too, who started the practice of marking syllables to be accented.

One of the greatest of all lexicographers (dictionary-makers) was Dr. Samuel Johnson, whose two-volume dictionary appeared in 1755. He wrote in the preface:

> When I took the first survey of my undertaking, I found our speech copious without order, and energetick without rules: wherever I turned my view, there was perplexity to be disentangled, and confusion to be regulated; choice was to be made out of boundless variety, without any established principle of selection; adulterations were to be detected, without a settled test of purity; and modes of expression to be rejected or received, without the suffrages [*support*] of any writers of classical reputation or acknowledged authority.

Johnson, then, hoped to bring some degree of regularity to the language, and to a degree he succeeded. Many words that had formerly been spelled in two or more ways were regularized, and certainly Johnson effected some clarification of meaning for hundreds of words. He also added to what was known about etymologies (although he was occasionally wrong), and his was one of the first dictionaries to indicate accent for pronunciation.

He based his definitions not on his own opinion but on the way that authors actually used words, and he included thousands of quotations to illustrate. Johnson thus began the procedure followed by respectable lexicographers ever since: gather many illustrative quotations for each word, and then examine the quotations to determine the meaning of the word. As a result of following this procedure, a modern dictionary publisher may have hundreds of filing cabinets filled with millions of "citation" cards bearing examples of word use.

Most of Dr. Johnson's definitions are straightforward (for example: MO'THERLY. *adj.* [from *mother* and *like*.] Belonging to a mother; suitable to a mother.), but a few have become famous because the good Doctor's personality shows through:

> *politician:* A man of artifice; one deep of contrivance.
> *patriotism:* The last refuge of a scoundrel.
> *lexicographer:* A writer of dictionaries, a harmless drudge that busies himself in tracing the original and detailing the significance of words.

Johnson's fondness for Latinisms was mentioned on page 145. He defined *cough,* for example, as "a convulsion of the lungs, vellicated by some sharp serosity."

One more great dictionary of British origin must be mentioned. This is the *Oxford English Dictionary,* usually known by its initials, *OED.* Seventy years in the making, this many-volumed work was not completed until 1928, after hundreds of people had labored on it. It is the greatest authority on the early uses and meanings of English words and on their etymologies. Sir William Craigie of the *OED* staff later came to the University of Chicago to prepare (with James R. Hulbert) a four-volume *Dictionary of American English on Historical Principles* (1944), which in turn was followed by Mitford M. Mathews's shorter *Dictionary of Americanisms* (1951). In all these dictionaries, as well as in the Merriam-Webster

Third New International Dictionary, the basic procedures established by Dr. Johnson were followed, although of course refinements were made.

► Suppose that you are an employee of a dictionary publisher and that as one of your responsibilities you have to prepare the entry for *automation.* (Choose a different word if you prefer.) Suppose there are in the files about a hundred citations using this word. In writing the entry, how will you make decisions about questions like these?

a. How is the word divided into syllables?
b. How is it pronounced?
c. What part of speech is it?
d. What is its etymology?
e. Is there to be a single definition or more than one?
f. If more than one, in what order are the definitions to be presented?
g. If the citations show different spellings, which form or forms will you use in the entry?
h. Which quotations will you use as illustrations?

► Now you actually are to write an entry, for a proposed dictionary of modern slang. Choose a slang term that only recently has come into use in your school. Gather examples of its use in sentences, and prepare the dictionary entry by following the steps suggested by the questions above. (You may not be able to provide the etymology.)

7

english
around
the
world

1. How English Spread

THE spirit of adventure and conquest that brought Angles, Saxons, Jutes, Danes, and Normans to the British Isles remained alive in their descendants. King Henry VII in 1497 and 1498 sponsored explorations by John Cabot, the Italian navigator, whose discovery of the North American continent led to British claims on land in the New World. Other adventurers found their way to India and the "Spice Islands" by going through the Mediterranean and across Asia Minor, or by sailing around the southern tip of Africa and then northeastward.

In 1607, in the New World territory that Sir Walter Raleigh had named Virginia, the first successful

English colony was established, and in 1620 the Pilgrims settled in what is now Massachusetts. Between 1630 and 1640 sixteen thousand Puritans expanded the settlement of New England, and fifty thousand other Englishmen migrated to North America and the West Indies. A colony was established in Guiana, South America. The New World not only produced shipments of gold and furs for England, but also introduced white potatoes, sweet potatoes, tomatoes, corn, sugar, coffee, cocoa, and tobacco. Such evidence of wealth and novelty across the seas caused still more Englishmen to seek their fortunes abroad. A book called *Principal Navigations of English Seamen*, better known as Hakluyt's *Voyages*, aroused further interest.

Eventually England had colonies on every continent, including the whole of Australia as a Dominion. The land area of Canada, another Dominion, is about as large as that of the United States, and India, also formerly a British Dominion, occupies most of the huge subcontinent of Asia. Other British settlements were scattered through Africa and on islands in most of the oceans. It was a proud boast, before the colonies were lost one by one, that "the sun never sets on the British Empire."

▶ Members of your class may be asked to prepare reports on John Cabot, Sir Martin Frobisher, Sir Francis Drake, Sir Humphrey Gilbert, Sir Walter Raleigh, the Pilgrim settlement at Plymouth, the British East India Company, and British settlements in Australia, Canada, India, or elsewhere.

Besides exploration and colonization, other influences were at work in spreading the language. One was the increasingly large number of books published in England. These gave the people—more and more of whom were learning to read—the opportunity to increase their interest in foreign lands, and the reading of English books by foreigners spread the language in other countries.

Missionaries, many times from France or Spain but sometimes from England, often lived with groups of natives and taught them some English so that they could read the Bible, although occasionally it seemed easier to translate parts of the Bible into the native languages. Such translation often posed special problems. The Eskimos, for example, had no word for *sheep,* so "the lamb of God" might have to be translated "the baby seal of God." The Hindi and Urdu languages of India and Pakistan have no verb that is the equivalent of *have,* one of the most used in English. Chinese has no word for *yes* or *no,* and *t'a* does duty for *he, she,* and *it.* And, as Gary Jennings tells us in his fascinating *Personalities of Language:*

> . . . Numerous heathens recoil at the idea of a "kiss," so the Bibles supplied to them render the word in such ways as "to greet by smelling each other's face." A "temple," in a society that never heard of such a thing, may become a "praise-God house." The idea of "worship" is conveyed to one Central American tribe as "to wag one's tail before God."[1]

---

[1]Gary Jennings, *Personalities of Language,* New York: Thomas Y. Crowell Co., 1965, p. 35.

The development of the United States into a power-ful nation of the world speeded up the use of English in other lands. American automobile manufacturers, for instance, buy materials from all parts of the world, and foreigners who do business with Americans find it useful to know their language. Hundreds of American corporations have offices abroad. Americans travel overseas a great deal, and their hosts in other lands like to be able to talk with them. American movies have long been shown in thousands of foreign theaters, and even though subtitles are added, the moviegoers hear the American voices and pick up phrases, at least. Many American soldiers are stationed abroad and often become friendly with the residents. Sometimes American textbooks are used in other countries. So, inevitably, American influence has acquainted millions of people with the American version of the English language.

The increase in population in English-speaking lands also obviously resulted in more speakers of the language. In 1066 there were probably only about one and a half million English, and this number had approximately tripled by the age of Shakespeare. But by 1971 the United Kingdom had a population of over fifty-five million, a growth of about 1100 per-cent in only three and a half centuries.

Here are population figures for the 1970's in other lands where English is the major language:[2]

Australia	13,026,300
Canada	21,850,000
Ireland	3,010,000
New Zealand	2,909,916

[2]Taken from the 1974 edition of *Information Please Almanac*, New York: Simon and Schuster, pp. 319–320.

| South Africa | 22,990,000 |
| United States | 203,235,298 |

But these figures tell only part of the story. English is one of the leading languages in India, Pakistan, and a large number of other nations or territories. In addition, many millions of persons around the world learned their native language as infants, but later in school or through private study learned some English as well. In the Scandinavian countries, for instance, almost all school children are required by law to study English, since those countries are dependent upon import and export business, and English is the leading language for international commerce. English is the most widely taught foreign language in Russia and in most other European countries. Japan is said to have eighty thousand *teachers* of English. Battles have erupted in India, and people have been killed, over the question of the status of English as an official language in that land of many languages.

Probably close to 350,000,000 people today have English as their native language. At least as many more are somewhat familiar with it—can read it or speak it or at least use it to a limited extent. A total, then, of perhaps 700,000,000 of the earth's inhabitants possess some degree of skill in English. This is almost a fourth of the world's population.

It is interesting to note that besides the enormous number who have some degree of skill in English, there are many others with a minimal acquaintance— people of Europe and Asia whose languages have borrowed from English, just as English so often has borrowed from other languages. On the next page are a few of the borrowings, some that have been adopted into the standard languages, others from Pidgins.

bifuteki (Japanese)
biru (Japanese)
dansu (Japanese)
disukaunto-hausu (Japanese)
kosuchumu jueru (Japanese)
naifu (Japanese)
napukin (Japanese)
pikunikku (Japanese)
bifteck (French)
bouledogue (French)

coctel (Spanish)
huachar (Spanish)
colcrem (Italian)
futbol (Italian)
pulova (Italian)
tegedizi (Italian)
tumorro (Italian)
p'u k'e (Chinese)
te lu fêng (Chinese)
yu meh (Chinese)

► See whether you can figure out the English words before you look at the answers in the footnote.[3] Pronouncing the words aloud may help.

2. Variations in English

English doesn't sound quite the same the world over. In the British Isles alone there are some twenty fairly distinct dialects, and the United States has three major dialects (Northern, Midland, and Southern) as well as a large number of subdialects or local variations. The speech of Philadelphia, for example, is noticeably different from that of Pittsburgh.

[3]The English words are *beefsteak, beer, dance, discount house, costume jewelry, knife, napkin, picnic, beefsteak, bulldog, cocktail* (which the French often spell *coquetel*), *to watch, cold cream, football, pullover, take it easy, tomorrow, poker, telephone, humor.* How many did you guess?

A resident of the United States can often identify a Canadian by small differences in pronunciation, vocabulary, or usage. South African English has been influenced by Afrikaans, the widely spoken South African Dutch, and by native African languages.

Australian English sounds somewhat like London Cockney, a quite natural development, since many of the early settlers were Cockneys. In addition, it has adopted and adapted a number of words from native tribes. The unofficial national anthem of Australia is "Waltzin' Matilda," which was immensely popular in the United States during World War II. The "Matilda" in the song is the pack carried by the jolly "swagman," a wandering worker. He is camped beside a "billabong," or water hole, in the shade of a "coolibah" tree. If he puts some food into his Matilda, the pack will sway and be "waltzin'" along on his back. Along comes a "jumbuck," a sheep, which the swagman kills and stuffs into the Matilda. But just then the "squatter," the owner of the ranch, comes along with troopers, who ask about the contents of the "tucker-bag." The swagman, trying to get away, jumps into the billabong and is drowned, but his ghost may still be heard singing "Waltzin' Matilda."

► If a recording of "Waltzin' Matilda" is available, your class will enjoy hearing it and comparing Australian with American English.

"Pidgin English" is widely used in many South Pacific islands and here and there throughout the

Orient. The name *Pidgin*, which originated in southern China, is derived from a distorted Chinese pronunciation of *business*. The name is most appropriate, since Pidgin is widely used for business dealings between natives and foreigners. Actually there are a number of varieties of Pidgin English (as well as Pidgin French and other Pidgin languages).

► Try to translate the following examples of Melanesian Pidgin into standard English. If you get stuck, the footnote provides the answers.

    a. smolfela haus
    b. bigfela haus
    c. badfela man
    d. gudfela meri
        (*Meri*, based on *Mary*, is "woman.")
    e. meri bilong man
    f. Mi luk.
    g. Mi lukim meri.
    h. Em i-lukim wol bilong haus.
        (*Em*, based on *him*, is "he.")
    i. Disfela haus i-bigfela.
    j. Em i-ridum buk.[4]

Mario Pei gives the following additional examples of Pidgin:

[4]These phrases and sentences are based on books about Pidgin by Robert A. Hall, Jr. Here are the translations: a. small house b. big house c. bad man d. good woman e. man's wife f. I look (*or* I see). g. I see the woman. h. He looks at the wall of the house. i. This house is big. j. He reads a book.

kill-'im-stink-fella (disinfectant)

Belly-belong-me-walk-about-too-much. (I have a
stomach ache.)

Put clothes belong-a table. (Set the table.)

Pei also tells of a Solomon Islands chieftain who re-
acted to New York City in this way: "Me look um
big fella place. He high up too much. He alla same one
fella mountain."[5]

Gary Jennings retells the New Guinea native's
description of a piano: "Him big-fella box, you fight
'im, 'e cry." "Halt or I'll fire" becomes "You-fella
you stand fast. You no can walkabout. Suppose you-
fella walkabout me kill 'im you long musket." A
policeman may be "gubmint catchum-fella," and
whiskers are "grass belong face." And in a wedding
ceremony for a Danish sailor and a Chinese girl the
English consul asked the girl, "This man wantchee
take you home-side makee wife-pidgin. Can do, no
can do?" Her reply, of course, was "Can do."[6]

The English spoken in various foreign countries
does not sound just alike, so we refer to a "German
accent," a "French accent," etc. The chief reason for
such accents is the tendency to pronounce English
vowels and consonants in the same way they are
pronounced in the speaker's native language. So a
German *w* has a *v* sound. A Spaniard may say "I
theenk" for *I think* because in Spanish such an *i*
is pronounced "ee." A Frenchman may say "ze" for
the because the voiced *th* is not used in French (or
in some other European languages). The well-known

[5]Pei, *op. cit.*, p. 168.
[6]Jennings, *op. cit.*, p. 190.

difficulties that Chinese and Japanese speakers have with *r* or *l* are caused by the lack of those precise sounds in their languages. Such varieties of pronunciation are often rather pleasing, and certainly are no worse than an American's attempts to pronounce the sounds of German, Spanish, French, or other languages.

To a foreign student, English poses problems besides pronunciation. Many languages, such as Japanese, have no word used like our *the,* and as a result a Japanese has great difficulty in deciding whether to use *the, a, an,* or nothing at all in a sentence like "Boy goes to school." Prepositions like *of, to, at,* and *in* are used in what foreigners consider an almost endless variety of situations. And problems with vocabulary are numerous. For example, a horse may be *fast* on the track, but the meaning is quite different if the horse is *fast* in a wire fence. One foreigner thanked an American lady for a "worthless" gift, not knowing that for some strange reason *worthless* and *priceless* are opposite in meaning. Obviously a person learning any foreign language will encounter difficulties, but English poses no less than its full share.

▶ What other examples of words can you think of that would probably puzzle a foreigner trying to use the language? What should you do if you hear a foreign-born speaker make a mistake in word usage?

When foreign students try to write English, they are troubled by spelling. (So are American students!)

Kite, fight, and *indict* all end in an "ite" sound, but only one is spelled with *ite*. Since *time* and *thyme* are pronounced the same, one would logically expect them to be spelled the same. Silent letters, as in *debt* and *island* and *psychology,* cause trouble. If English spelling were like that of Finnish or Spanish, with each word spelled as it is pronounced, it would definitely be easier to learn. But so far, all attempts at a full-scale reform have failed, largely because genuine reform would require an alphabet of at least forty letters, and different typewriters and typesetting machines, as well as reading lessons for every adult and child, since the new alphabet would make the language look quite strange. Even with such an alphabet, whose pronunciation should be chosen as the basis for spelling? If I say "haht cawfee" and you say "hawt cahfee," should the spelling reflect your sounds or mine?

► What are some of the special problems that you have in spelling? Look at some words that you have recently misspelled or seen misspelled. What parts of those words cause trouble? To what extent are the troubles caused by peculiarities of the language?

► What arguments in favor of spelling reform can you think of? What are some arguments against spelling reform besides those suggested above?

3. An International Language?

For centuries many people have longed for an international language so that a person could talk with or write to almost anybody in the world and be understood. At one time people who knew Latin could travel abroad and find in many countries other people who also knew Latin and could be addressed in that language. But in those days few people went to school, so the number who knew Latin was small.

In the seventeenth, eighteenth, and nineteenth centuries many men tried to construct artificial languages. In 1887 a Polish physician and language scholar named L. L. Zamenhof published "An International Language, by Dr. Esperanto" (a word that means "one who hopes" in the language that since has been called Esperanto). Zamenhof believed that if people shared a language, wars and other conflicts would be reduced because people would understand one another better.

Esperanto is a language based on elements common to European languages, including Latin. The language is completely regular. For instance, every noun ends in *o*, every adjective in *a*, every adverb in *e*. The prefix *mal-* makes a word into its opposite; thus *bona* is "good" and *malbona* "bad." Every present-tense verb ends in *as*, every past-tense verb in *is*.

Although there have been many publications in Esperanto, and although there are today about half a million scattered people who use it, it has never become widely adopted. Reformed versions, including Ido and Nov-Esperanto, have been no more successful. Neither have other artificial languages con-

structed at various times—Volapük, Novial, Inter-
lingua, and many more.

▶ What do you think of the idea of a constructed
artificial language for use as a supplement to one's
native language? If courses in Esperanto or some such
language were available in your school, would you be
likely to enroll? Why, why not, or under what condi-
tions?

▶ Some members of the class may be asked to prepare
reports on Esperanto, Volapük, or artificial languages
in general.

▶ A nineteenth-century Frenchman, J. F. Sudre,
devised a language called Solresol, composed entirely of the notes of the musical scale, which Sudre
listed as *do, re, mi, fa, sol, la, si. Dore milasi domi*
meant "I love you." This language could be played
on the piano as well as spoken. What advantages and
disadvantages do you see in a language with only
seven syllables? Another artificial language, Timerio,
consisted of written numbers. *1-80-17* meant "I love
you." Again, discuss the advantages and disadvantages.

Some people have argued that because a constructed language is an artificial one with no native

speakers, it is never likely to become popular as a universal language. They say that some widely used "natural" language is preferable, such as Chinese, Russian, French, Spanish, or English. The best such language would be one with a simple grammar, simple spelling, ease of pronunciation for many millions of speakers, a limited but adequate vocabulary, and a large number of speakers.

All five of the languages mentioned are strong in some of these respects, weak in others. Chinese has a simple grammar, but its differences in tone (see page 20) make it hard for a nonnative to pronounce, and its written characters are extremely time-consuming to learn. Russian and Spanish are easy to spell, but their grammars are complex. French, too, has a fairly complex grammar, and its spelling and pronunciation do not harmonize well. The grammar of English is relatively simple, but its spelling is difficult. All five languages have large numbers of speakers, but none has a very limited vocabulary, with English having the largest vocabulary of all.

► Suppose that wide agreement was reached that a second language should be taught to almost everybody in the world, to be used for all communications with "foreigners." Suppose also that a language other than English was chosen. Analyze your personal reactions to being required to learn Russian, say, or Chinese.

► What advantages and disadvantages do you now see in having one of the major existing languages as an international language? As a class, make a two-column list of these pros and cons. Do the advantages or the disadvantages seem stronger?

One attempt to make it easier for foreigners to learn English as a second language was the invention of Basic English, which was designed primarily for use as an international auxiliary language. The letters in *Basic* stand for *British, American, Scientific, International, Commercial*—words that describe its scope. Developed in 1926 to 1930 by British semanticist and psychologist Charles K. Ogden, Basic was recommended by such world figures as British Prime Minister Winston Churchill and American President Franklin D. Roosevelt.

Basic English has only 850 words: 600 nouns, 150 adjectives, and 100 "operational words." Those who favor Basic say that a reasonably intelligent person can master the language fairly well in only about fifty hours of study. They also say that the 850 words allow enough flexibility to make almost any sentence possible. Opponents of Basic, however, point out that Churchill could not have referred to "blood, sweat, and tears," since Basic has no word *sweat* or *tear;* in Basic, Churchill would have had to say "blood, body liquid, and eye water." Shakespeare's "Hark! Hark! the lark at heaven's gate sings" might have to be phrased, according to satirist Richard L. Greene, in this way:

> Listen! Listen! The small song bird at the doorway of God's living place makes a whistling sound on a high note.

► In its article on Basic English the *Encyclopaedia Britannica* lists all 850 words. Some members of the class may be asked to try to compose sentences in Basic, using only words from the list and following the Basic English rules.

► Your class may be asked to discuss the usefulness and the limitations of Basic. Do the criticisms of its opponents seem to you valid or invalid? fair or unfair?

The question of whether Basic English will ever indeed become an international auxiliary language cannot be answered. Nor can the question of whether "regular" English will continue to spread until finally it becomes customary for almost everyone in the world to learn English in addition to his native tongue. One person who thinks this may and should happen is Professor William F. Marquardt, a well-known linguist, who wrote a few years ago:

It is spoken as a native language by more than 270 million persons [today closer to 350 million] in such strategically dispersed countries as Great Britain, the United States, New Zealand, Australia, Ireland, the Republic of South Africa. It is used as an official language in some thirty other nations situated on every continent. It is the language most essential to military operations in most countries of the world. Knowledge of it is one of the surest ways to advancement in government, business or education in most non-English-speaking countries. There are more publications in English in the fields of science, technology, education, politics and literature than in any other language. It is the common language of aviation, and the one most used in international conferences, commerce, travel, the United Nations. It is currently being taught in more schools in non-English-speaking countries than any other language. Some 70 percent of the world's mail is written in English. More people speak it as a second language than any other, and more *literate* persons speak it than any other.[7]

It may be added that in some South American countries lessons in English are broadcast over loudspeakers in the town squares, where people sit on park benches to listen and learn. Many of the world's newspapers carry daily English lessons; when a lesson was accidentally left out in a newspaper of India one day, the paper received over five hundred letters of protest. The United States government has sponsored the preparation of English textbooks for use abroad, and for a number of years the Russians and the Communist Chinese have prepared English textbooks (with built-in propaganda against "American imperialism"). In short, there is much evidence that English may indeed be becoming the world's major auxiliary language.

But it would be unwise to make any flat predictions. The difficulty of English spelling, as we have noted,

[7]Quoted in Jennings, *op. cit.*, pp. 247–248.

discourages many learners. So does the fact that many pronunciations do not conform closely to the spellings. (A well-known example is the pronunciation of *enough, cough, bough, though, through;* if *enough* is pronounced "enuff," why shouldn't the others be "kuff," "buff," "thuff," and "thruff"?) Moreover, the English vocabulary is so huge that even native speakers can master no more than a fraction of the words; this very hugeness tends to discourage learners.

In addition, we must keep in mind that the other great nations of the world are not especially eager for English to be understood in every village of the earth. Indeed, if the speakers of another language were to take over world leadership in commerce, in military power, and/or in science (unlikely as this is), that language might well become the one that most people would want to learn instead of English.

Despite all this, however, and although there is no absolute assurance that it will happen, English has an excellent chance of becoming the chief auxiliary language of the world.

► Many people have argued that if everybody in the world could speak the same language, understanding would be greater and war less likely. Discuss whether you agree with this statement or not—and why.

► Do you think English is a good choice or a poor choice as an international language? Be ready to give specific reasons to support your answer.

APPENDIX

*A Translation of
the Story of Ohthere (page 63)*

Ohthere said to his lord, King Alfred, that of all Northmen he lived farthest north. He said that he lived in the northern land by the West Sea [perhaps near the Arctic Circle]. He said, though, that the land stretches very far north from there, yet it is all waste except that Finns camp in a few places here and there, for hunting in winter and for fishing in the sea in summer.

He said that at one time he wanted to find how far straight north the land lay, or whether any people lived north of the wasteland. Then [So] he went northward along the land. All the way, for three days, he kept the wasteland on the starboard and the open sea on the larboard. Then he was as far north as the farthest whalehunters go. Then he went still northward as far as he might sail in the next three days. Then the land there turned straight east, or the sea [turned in] on the land, he did not know which; but he knew that he waited there for west and somewhat northerly winds, and then sailed east along the land as far as he might in four days. Then he had to wait there for a straight north wind because the land turned straight south there, or the sea [turned in] on the land, he did not know which. Then he sailed from there straight south near the land, as far as he might in five days. Then there lay a great river up in that land. Then they turned around at the river, because they did not dare to sail past it on account of hostility, for that land was all inhabited on the other side of the river. He had not previously encountered any inhabited land since he left his own home. Instead, all the way there was wasteland on the starboard, except for fishermen and fowlers and hunters, and they were all Finns; and on the larboard he had the open sea.

1 2 3 4 5 6 7 8 9 10 11 12 13 14 15 16 17 18 19 20 21 22 23 24 25 GBC 82 81 80 79 78 77 76 75 74